# The Romance of Language

By
**Alethea Chaplin**
B.A. Lond.

Author of "The Rose Book of Romance," "General Knowledge Papers," "A Treasury of Verse for Little Ones," etc.

PLATE I—THE ROSETTA STONE.

*[Frontispiece*

TO
MY MOTHER

# PREFACE

TRULY the path of the student of language is beset with pitfalls, and it behoves him to walk warily lest he be accused of rushing in where he should fear to tread. But there can be no discovery without enterprise and no master so good as a mistake corrected, and he who sets out on this journey can be sure of adventures.

My aim, however imperfectly achieved, has been not to attempt the impossible—the making of discoveries—but to awaken in the minds of senior students an interest in the most humane of sciences and to develop and enforce the truth of Emerson's remark that every word was once a poem which is well worth reading.

Unlike many sciences, the study of languages entails no expensive outfit, but is free as the sun and air to all who will but read, mark, learn, and inwardly digest the materials that lie to hand.

Ruskin, speaking in his *Sesame and Lilies* of the right study of language, says that every well-educated man must know the "*peerage* of words" and be sure of their right meaning.

In a book such as this much must of necessity be omitted—I have tried merely to point out the way to this right knowledge of words in the most interesting directions and have avoided any discussion of opposing theories.

If one person only should enjoy the reading half as much as I have enjoyed the preparation of this book and should be thereby encouraged to study further the Romance of Language, I should feel repaid.

I have to acknowledge my profound indebtedness not only to all those whose works I have consulted, but especially to one friend, and to Mr. J. G. Grattan (Lecturer in Old English at University College, London) for his help and criticism.

A. C.

# CONTENTS

## CHAPTER I

THE BIRTH AND GROWTH OF LANGUAGE . . 1

The Mother Language—Development of Daughter Languages—Asiatic and European Branches.

## CHAPTER II

WRITING AND THE ALPHABET . . . 26

The Beginnings of Writing—Four Stages—Cuneiform, Hieroglyphic, and Other Scripts.

## CHAPTER III

ENGLISH IN THE MAKING . . . . 54

The Contributions of Other Tongues towards the Growth of Standard English.

## CHAPTER IV

THE GROWTH OF ENGLISH . . . . 75

Change from Synthetic to Analytic Language—Early, Middle, and Modern English.

# CONTENTS

## CHAPTER V

SOME ANOMALIES IN ENGLISH . . . 117

Words that have suffered Change—Others that have travelled far and had Adventures.

## CHAPTER VI

METAPHOR IN EVERYDAY SPEECH . . . 137

Connected with the Sea, War, Archery, Animals, Colours, etc.

## CHAPTER VII

PLACE NAMES . . . . . . 155

How they Support the Evidence of History—Words of Geographical Origin.

## CHAPTER VIII

PERSONAL NAMES . . . . . . 179

Origin—Distribution of Surnames in England—Words Coined from Personal Names.

## CHAPTER IX

NATIONAL CHARACTER AND LANGUAGE . . 193

Character of Aryans, Romans, and Anglo-Saxons as shown in their Language.

BIBLIOGRAPHY . . . . . . 229

INDEX . . . . . . . . 233

# LIST OF ILLUSTRATIONS

PLATE

I. THE ROSETTA STONE . . *Frontispiece*

A black basalt slab, approximately 3 ft. by 2 ft. 6 ins., with inscription in hieratic and demotic Egyptian and uncial Greek, discovered near Rosetta in 1798, and now in the British Museum. This slab gave the key to the interpretation of the Egyptian hieroglyphic writing. (See pp. 41-3.)

FACING PAGE

II. CAVE DRAWING . . . . . 4

Piece of bone with scratches representing a horse's head, found in Robin Hood Cave, Creswell Crags, Derbyshire, and now in the British Museum. Many better examples of cave drawings than this have been found in other countries, especially in France, but it seemed preferable to reproduce a native example, and one that is less well known. For greater clearness the object has been enlarged in reproduction. The original is about $2\frac{1}{2}$ ins. in length. (See pp. 3-4.)

III. THE PENN WAMPUM . . . 30

The belt is made of white shell-beads, with the figures interwoven in violet-coloured beads. The dark line at the right-hand end is due to some of the beads being missing. Reproduced by kind permission of the Historical Society of Pennsylvania, from a photograph by C. S. Bradford. (See pp. 30-1.)

# LIST OF ILLUSTRATIONS

PLATE                                                                   FACING PAGE

IV. INDIAN PICTOGRAPH . . . . . 34

    A petition sent by a group of Indian Chippewa tribes, of the region of L. Superior, to the United States Congress in 1849, asking for the retrocession of some territories which the tribe had formerly ceded to the United States. Reproduced from a drawing in H. R. Schoolcraft's *Information respecting the History, Condition, etc., of the Indian Tribes of the United States*, 1851, etc., vol. i. The numerical references (which are, of course, not in the original) are as follows. Nos. 1-7 are the totems of the petitioning tribe or clans, namely a crane, three martens, a bear, a man-fish (a mythical fish corresponding with the merman of Europe), and a cat-fish. No. 8 the small Rice Lakes, the grant of which was desired. No. 9 the path from Lake Superior to the territories. Nos. 10 and 11 Lake Superior. The original drawing seems to be now untraceable. The publishers have to thank the authorities of the Library of Congress and the Office of Indian Affairs at Washington, for their assistance in attempting to discover where it now is. (See p. 33.)

V. CUNEIFORM INSCRIPTION . . . . 40

    Part of the Obelisk of Shalmaneser II, King of Assyria, about 860 B.C., inscribed with the annals of the king and a series of reliefs illustrating the receiving of tribute from conquered nations. Now in the British Museum. (See pp. 35-9.)

VI. AN ILLUMINATED MANUSCRIPT OF THE
    FIFTEENTH CENTURY . . . . 64

    A page from a French manuscript, "Hours of the Virgin," now in the British Museum (Harley MS. 2952). (See pp. 46-8.)

LIST OF ILLUSTRATIONS xiii

| PLATE | | FACING PAGE |
|---|---|---|

VII. A Horn-book . . . . . . . 96

Sixteenth or early seventeenth-century horn-book, in oak frame measuring 9½ ins. by 5 ins. The horn covering is partly broken away. From the British Museum. (See pp. 49-50.)

VIII. Knife with Runic Alphabet or "Futhorc" . . . . . 128

Sword-knife, or scramasax, with Runic alphabet inlaid in brass and silver. Found in the Thames, and now in the British Museum. The whole knife measures about 2 ft. by 1½ ins., but only the central portion (about 10 ins.) is here reproduced. (See pp. 51-2.)

IX. Ogam Inscription . . . . . 160

A stone pillar, 6 ft. high, with the name of Maccutrenus Saliciduni in Ogam characters and Latin letters, from Cray, Brecknockshire. The Ogam inscription is, as usual, cut on two adjacent faces, the edge between them serving as a base line. The dots and strokes forming the alphabet have different values according as they are on one side or the other of the base line or across it. (See p. 52.)

X. The Ruthwell Cross . . . . 208

A stone cross which now stands in an apse within the Parish Church of Ruthwell, Dumfriesshire. It is 18 ft. in height, and dates from the seventh or eighth century. It has Latin inscriptions on the front and back, enclosing sculptured panels from the life of our Lord and from early church history. Upon the sides, in Runic letters, is to be seen part of the "Dream of the Holy Rood," an Anglo-Saxon poem ascribed to Cædmon. Owing to the comparatively small size of the inscription, it is

xiv                LIST OF ILLUSTRATIONS

impossible to show this in the reproduction. It runs along the edges and across the monument at the sides of the sculptured panels. Reproduced by kind permission of Messrs. J. Maxwell & Son, of Dumfries, from a photograph by Mr. R. Dinwiddie. (See pp. 81-2.)

## ILLUSTRATIONS IN THE TEXT

       PAGE

SKETCH-MAP OF EUROPE . . . . . 12

    Showing the Descendants of the Mother Tongue.

SKETCH-MAP OF THE BRITISH ISLES . . . 169

    Showing the localities occupied by the Norwegians, Celts, Danes, and Anglo-Saxons.

# THE ROMANCE OF LANGUAGE

## CHAPTER I

### THE BIRTH AND GROWTH OF LANGUAGE

WHEN you have been reading, writing, or speaking—that is, when you have been using words—have you ever stopped short and asked yourself how it is that we speak and write as we do—how it is that the words we use came to have the meaning we now attach to them—how it is that our English language is different from the speech of other nations—in fact, have you ever wondered how our language grew to be the wonderful thing it is?

Possibly not, but, even if you have, perhaps you will look into the matter a little more closely now and follow with me the marvellous adventures of some of our everyday words which, since they were born, have travelled far and in many countries, worn many dresses, and changed their appearance so much that their Mother Language would hardly know them.

If you will do this, I think that, at the end of the journey, you will be ready to acknowledge that the adventures of many words are just as exciting as those of knights and heroes of old, and that we can quite truthfully speak of the "Romance of Language."

As for the birth of language we know nothing about it, for that event took place so long ago that all is wrapped in mystery. Just as all the arts and sciences have developed from the natural needs of man to get food and provide a shelter from the extremes of heat and cold, so, from the fact that man is a social animal, we gather that very early in his career he must have found some sort of language necessary to enable him to communicate with his fellows.

It will give us a little idea of the antiquity of language if we suggest that it was born long before the time of some very early people called the Cave Dwellers, who lived perhaps forty thousand years ago, when the world was much colder than it is now. Traces of these people who lived in caves have been found in many countries, France, Belgium, Greenland, among others, and we know that they knew the use of fire, for the effects of it are still noticeable on the roofs and walls of their caves. They also burnt the fat of animals in stone lamps which have been found together with many of their stone weapons and tools and the bones of many animals probably killed for food.

# BIRTH AND GROWTH OF LANGUAGE 3

These people lived a hard, active life, hunting and fishing, and they knew strange animals that exist no longer, such as the mammoth, a huge creature something like an enormous elephant, whose bones have been dug up from time to time in various parts of the world. The hunters wore skins of animals sewn together by bone needles threaded with the sinews of the reindeer, and they sometimes lived in huts as well as caves.

But perhaps the most interesting fact about these Cave Dwellers is that they were very clever artists, as I think you will allow if you look at the reproductions of some of their drawings (see Plate II).

Often they drew on the walls of their caves, scratching the lines with hard bone or flint and then rubbing in some colouring matter which can still be plainly seen, the drawings being, as a rule, those of animals, reindeer, bison, wild horses in the warmer countries of France, Belgium, Spain; while in the colder northern lands we find pictures of whales, walruses, and seals.

These drawings are often wonderfully life-like, but the Cave Dwellers could do something still more clever—they could carve the most marvellous figures on bone, and you must remember that all this work was done with rude tools of flint and bone.

Now, if these people were as clever as this, it

seems almost certain that they had a fairly complete language, so that it must have been thousands of years before their time that speech began.

Though, however, we do not know much, or anything, of the beginnings of language, we can guess a great deal and learn much from studying primitive people and children, a method that is very useful when we want to understand beginnings.

How do animals make themselves understood, and children before they can talk ? By gestures—the cat rubs against you when she is pleased, and the dog wags his tail, while children naturally nod or shake their head when they want, or do not want, anything, and clap their hands and dance about when pleased, or kick and wriggle when angry or disappointed. Think, too, of deaf and dumb people, how well they make themselves understood by signs, just as people of different nationalities do when they have no common speech; while the various tribes of American Indians can make other tribes, speaking quite different languages, understand perfectly by means of gestures.

We English people use this language of gesture very little compared with some other nations, but even we know how much expression can be put into a wave of the hand, a lifting of the eyebrows, a shrug of the shoulders; and unconsciously add gesture to words as when we clap our hands, draw down the

PLATE II—CAVE DRAWING.

# BIRTH AND GROWTH OF LANGUAGE 5

corners of our mouth in disapproval, or beckon with our finger.

Again, we ask, how do children first learn to talk? and we know that they begin by imitating sounds and words repeated to them until they come to understand their meaning.

If we apply this to the people of early times, we can imagine them communicating with one another, first by signs—the natural gestures that go with certain feelings—the shudder of fear (the early people had much to fear from the wild animals that roamed about them), the open eyes of surprise, the dance and caper of delight when the hunter killed some specially troublesome enemy, or, again, the frown or threatening gesture of anger.

If we add to this use of gesture the natural exclamations that accompany any sudden emotion—the howl of pain, the cry of fear, the laughter of pleasure—then we have the beginnings of speech.

We cannot, of course, be sure that this was how language was born, but it seems probable that it began in some such way.

Imagine to yourself an early man, who could not yet speak, but who had seen some particularly fierce and terrible beast, feared by all his people. How could he warn his friends of the approach of such an enemy? Would it not be natural for him to roar if it were a lion, or hiss with a wriggling motion if it were a snake? By this means his companions would understand clearly what he wanted to express, and hide quickly or prepare to attack the enemy.

We cannot be sure, but this is how we think that "natural language," as distinct from "language proper," began, and once the start was made things soon progressed.

Having found that he had a voice, the early man would want to use it; he was probably proud of it and wished to show off his new accomplishment, and set to work to imitate all the sounds he heard—the cries of birds, the lowing of cattle, the rush of water, the whizzing sound of a stone flung into the air.

How most words came into being we can never tell, but of the origin of the class of words called *onomatopœic* we can certainly be fairly sure. These words are so called from the Greek words meaning "to make" and "a name," and are those which reproduce a sound, as *buzz, cuckoo, fizz*. There are several classes of onomatopœic words, all of which express some object or action that would have its place in the life of a primitive people.

Take, for instance, the names of animals, obviously formed from the noise they make, as *crow, pee-wit*, and the names for the noises themselves, *twitter, cackle, gobble, quack, coo, caw, croak, roar, yelp, neigh, hoot*, and the inarticulate human noises expressed by

# BIRTH AND GROWTH OF LANGUAGE 7

a sob, a sigh, a moan, a wail, a groan, a cough, a laugh, a whoop, a yawn, a shriek.

Sounds which all primitive people would often hear and which are coined into words are *bang, crack, creak, dash, splash, hum,* and those made by the collision of hard bodies as *clap, rap, snap, flap, crash, bang, drum, thump.* Does not the noise of a fire burning up suggest *crackle,* and the drip of the rain *patter* ?

Many words for " cutting " and the " object cut " seem to have been born in the same way and most of them contain the hissing *s* (from the noise produced in cutting a hard substance) together with *r* and the various vowels. We do not mean to say that all such words were known to primitive man or are strictly onomatopœic, but, that such was, in many cases, their origin, seems reasonably certain. Think of the following, all connected with cutting— *share, shear, scissors, shire, scythe, saw, scrape, shield, scour, sharp, scar.*

Is it again purely chance that such words as *fiend, foe, feud, filth, fear,* have the *f* sound of contempt as in *fie* ? and is there no significance in the natural movements of hands and especially of lips, which move outwards to say " go," but inwards to say " come " ? So for *me, us, I, our,* the lips are drawn slightly in, and for *you, they, their,* are pushed out away from the speaker.

Of course, it is only a small proportion of our words which are strictly onomatopœic; similarity of sound and association of ideas must account for many; often, again, the reason for the birth of some new word may have been very far-fetched, just as it is in the case of nicknames of to-day or of new slang words, whose origin is soon forgotten when the word has passed into the language. If we forget so soon, is it wonderful that we should have no clue to the real origin of most of our words that have existed for thousands and thousands of years?

The problem of why certain words should denote certain objects or actions will never be solved—why, for instance, *blue* is called *blue* and not *red*, or why a *rose* is called a *rose*, or a *house* a *house*; we must be content to take the words as we find them and trace their history back wherever possible to a certain point beyond which we cannot go, for their birth is wrapped in mystery.

You will notice that people seem naturally to coin new names on onomatopœic lines, as in the case of *puff-puff*, *hurdy-gurdy*, *fizzle*, *hooter*, *sizzle*; a fact which may perhaps support the theory that our primitive forefathers began with such words.

This idea may be said to run side by side with the theory that early man lived largely among the branches of trees, for a drowning man throws up his arms and clutches instinctively at the water as if it were something firm; and we all know that in moments of excitement primitive traits come out clearly, just as, though a man may have spoken a foreign tongue perfectly for years, at such times he falls back unconsciously into his mother tongue.

You have probably noticed that children invent for certain persons and things special sounds or names, which, by degrees, the people around them understand as describing those persons or objects to the child's mind, although in themselves the sounds have no real meaning. Boys and girls at school often invent for themselves a secret language which is quite meaningless to outsiders, an interesting example of this being the account that De Quincey gives in his *Autobiographical Sketches* of a language called *Ziph*, which was spoken at Eton.

Our early forefathers may have done as the baby does, and, by always uttering the same sound when pointing to a certain object or performing a certain action, they may have given birth to words which in time everyone came to understand. Thus would be born the names for most of the ordinary objects and everyday actions in the life of a primitive people, and, by slow degrees, those words would come to be applied to ideas, as, for example, the words " heat " or " fire " might be used of the heat of anger, or the word " see " of understanding or the seeing of the mind, so that language would grow and develop, though it would take thousands of years to become anything like the first language we know of.

Having thus seen briefly *how* language was probably born, we may ask ourselves *where* was it born ?

This, also, is a question we cannot answer definitely, as, at present anyhow, nobody knows. There were, of course, many varieties of early language, spoken by people living in the various parts of the world, but the one we are going to speak of is the parent of most of the European languages and therefore the one that interests us most nearly.

Scholars who have studied the question differ in opinion as to the probable birthplace of this tongue ; some years ago it was generally thought that it was first spoken in Asia and from there was brought into Europe, but now most authorities agree in thinking it was born in Europe, and there seems good reason for thinking its birthplace was on the plains of Central Europe or near the Baltic Sea, and that it was spoken as one complete or undivided language as far back as 10,000 B.C.

As, however, nobody really knows, and as the reasons for holding this theory are long and learned, we must be content to remain in doubt on this point, and we can quite well follow out the romance of language without knowing the precise place of its birth.

# BIRTH AND GROWTH OF LANGUAGE 11

We are not going to use a number of long words, but we will just mention two of the various names for this early tongue, though we shall not, generally, use either of them.

The two names are *Aryan* and *Indo-European*—*Aryan* originally meaning " noble," as the people of the early Aryan race considered themselves superior to the surrounding tribes ; and *Indo-European* meaning, of course, connected with India and Europe.

Now neither of these names is a very good one for this language, as the term " Aryan " is often used to mean the Asiatic branches only ; while " Indo-European " leaves out Persia, whose language belongs to this family. It will be simpler, then, for us to call this early tongue the *Mother Language,* for, as we shall see shortly, many daughter languages sprang from it, yes, and granddaughters and great-granddaughters.

As we are dealing with the subject rather fully in another chapter of this book, we will not stop to describe the Mother Language or say anything about the people who spoke it, but will pass on to the question as to how and in what directions it spread from its early home in the plains.

These early ancestors of ours did not always stay at home on their plain, wherever it was, but gradually migrated to the neighbouring countries, and from there still farther afield, gradually mixing with other

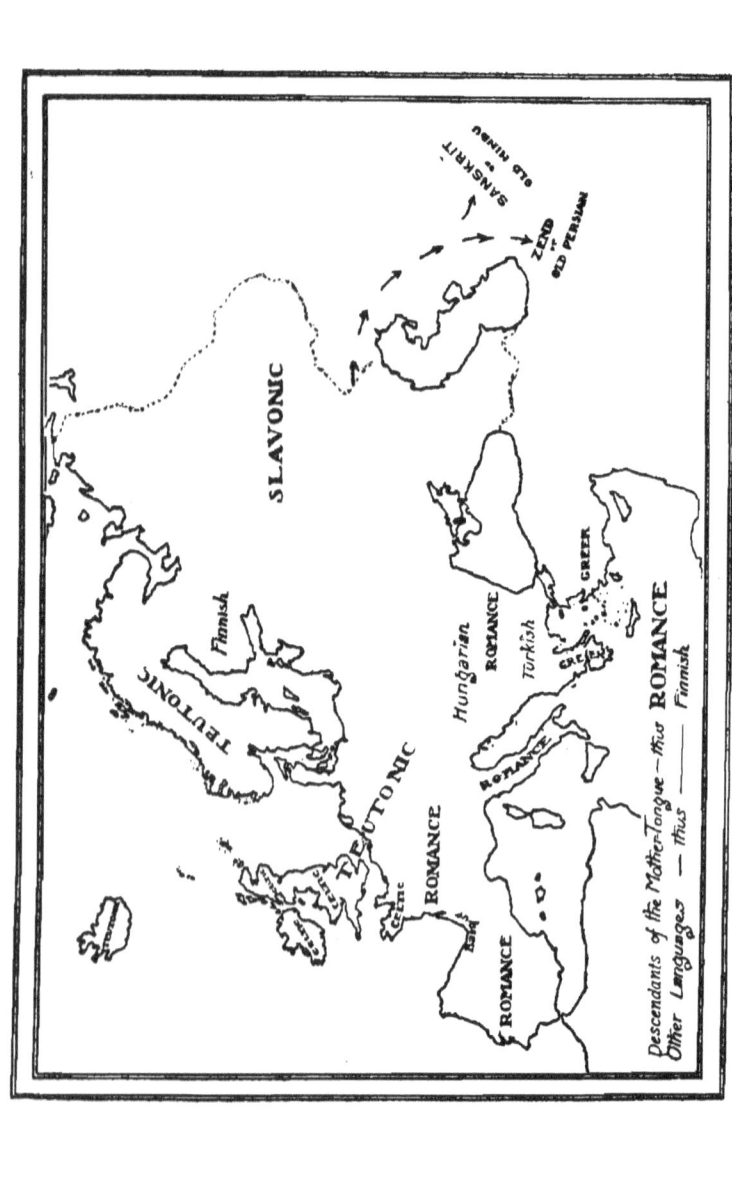

# BIRTH AND GROWTH OF LANGUAGE 13

TABLE OF DESCENDANTS OF THE MOTHER LANGUAGE

ASIATIC :
    *Sanskrit* or Old Hindu.
    *Zend* or Old Persian.

EUROPEAN :
    *Greek.*
    *Latin* with its daughters, the Romance Languages :
        Italian, Spanish, French, Portuguese, Roumanian.
    *Celtic* including Cymric (Welsh) ; Breton, Erse (Irish),
        Gaelic (Scottish), Manx.
    *Slavonic* or Baltic : Russian, Polish, Lithuanian.
    *Teutonic* : English, German, Norse.

THE TEUTONIC LANGUAGES ARE FURTHER SUBDIVIDED INTO :
    *Scandinavian* or Norse : Icelandic, Swedish, Norwegian,
        Danish.
    *Low German* : English, Dutch.
    *High German* : German.

---

peoples, borrowing words from them, living different lives under different conditions and so becoming less and less like the people they had left at home. And, as the people altered in their way of living and habits, so their language changed—foreign words were adopted, new names were coined to fit the new occupations and objects of a different life, so that by degrees the language they spoke would hardly be recognised as that of their fathers.

Now this change took place very slowly and not in one direction only, but in many, so that a number of variations or dialects of the Mother Tongue grew up, not, at first, very different from their parent, and the people from one part of a country could understand the speech of people from other parts. In some lands, however, as in Greece, where the country is cut up naturally into valleys, the people in one valley would gradually come to speak somewhat differently from those in other valleys whom they seldom, if ever, met because of the difficulties of crossing the mountains that divided them.

As time went on, the differences between the speech of one valley and another became more and more marked, until, by the time some of the people migrated to another country, they spoke a language very different from that of their fathers.

If you look at the table of languages on the previous page, you will see a list of those which are daughters of the Mother Tongue and the map will show you where the people live who speak those languages.

Just as there are in the world great languages such as Chinese or Hebrew, or Arabic, which are not descended from our Mother Tongue, so there are some less important, in Europe, that are outside this family, such, for instance, as the language of the gipsies and of the Basques who live on the coast of the Bay of Biscay, that of the Finns, of the Turks, and of the Hungarians.

Speaking, however, of the daughter languages of our family, we have in the Asiatic branch two so-

# BIRTH AND GROWTH OF LANGUAGE

called *dead* languages, because no longer spoken, namely, Sanskrit and Zend.

Sanskrit, or Old Hindu, is an extremely interesting language, and most useful to scholars who try to trace back words to their beginnings in the Mother Tongue, for they are often less changed in Sanskrit than anywhere else. In this language there exist poems, plays, and philosophical writings, and a collection of hymns called *Vedas,* which have a most romantic interest as being among the oldest known writings in the world.

*Veda* is from a Sanskrit word *vid,* " to know," which you will easily see is a relation of the Latin *videre,* " to see," and perhaps you will recognise its relationship to the old English words *wit* and *wist,* " know," which you have come across in the Bible.

There are four of these *Vedas* or collections of sacred writings, but the best known is the *Rig-Veda* (*rig* = " praise " or " celebration "), and it is also the most interesting and contains hymns and prayers used by the priests in their sacrifices and services. These hymns were probably *composed* about eight centuries before Christ, but were not *written down* till about two centuries after Christ, so that you see for ten centuries they lived unwritten—carried in the memories of the priests, who learned them by heart and handed them down from generation to generation.

In these hymns the priests worship one God, whose spirit dwells in the forces of nature, so that we find hymns and prayers to the sun, the fire, the water—the wind and the thunder are the voice of God; and man loves the birds, the trees, the sky, and the humble joys of life, thanking God for His gifts.

The people who composed these hymns and of whom we read in the Vedas were in a much higher state of civilisation than those who used the Mother Language even in its latest form, and their speech had developed and become rich and full of meaning.

If you look on the map of Europe, you will find, near Poland, a country called Lithuania, which is particularly interesting because its people speak, even now, a language which is more like Sanskrit than any other we know, and therefore it is very closely related to the Mother Tongue. Not only is the language primitive, but the people themselves are simple in their habits and ideas, being peasants engaged in tending flocks and herds, tilling the ground in primitive fashion and keeping bees as their early ancestors did. They are slow and sleepy of temperament, with fair hair and blue eyes, strongly built, but not very active; simple and superstitious in their beliefs—in fact, they are very much as we imagine the early people to have been, who spoke the Mother Language, living, as they do, far from the march of civilisation in their marshy lowland home.

# BIRTH AND GROWTH OF LANGUAGE 17

Old Persian or Zend, like Sanskrit, is interesting because in this language we have some very early writings, also hymns—the hymns of the old fire-worshippers of Persia, which in their collected form are called *Avestas* or *Zend-Avestas*, which means " the authorised version and commentary." The language in which they are written is something like Sanskrit, and therefore, by studying both tongues together, we can often trace words back to the form they had in the Mother Language. Both these Asiatic branches of the early family apparently moved eastwards together, one going farther than the other, and their languages have a great deal in common though naturally showing differences such as we have seen arose in the European daughter tongues.

Below we give a few words which have passed into many of the daughter languages—in some cases you will not be able to trace the relationship so clearly as in others, but, allowing for the regular interchange of letters (chiefly of consonants) in the passage of words from one language to another, you will be able to see the likeness of the English forms to those in the Sanskrit and other languages.

| *Sanskrit* | *Latin* | *German* | *English* |
|---|---|---|---|
| hanser | anser (= hanser) | gans | goose |
| vah (to carry) | vehere | wagon, weg | wain, way |
| uda | unda | wasser | water |
| bhrâtr | frater | bruder | brother |
| nîda | nidus | nest | nest |

In looking at this list you must remember that letters changed in sound in passing from one language to another, these changes taking place quite regularly according to definite rules, called sound laws.

These laws relate very largely to consonants and explain why the words *goose* and *brother*, given above, appear with a different initial consonant in the various languages, and so look more changed than they really are.

But to return to the *Avestas*.

We do not possess all the books that were once composed, we cannot say *written*, for, like the *Vedas*, they were handed down by word of mouth for many centuries, but some of those now in existence were composed by a famous early Persian teacher, Zoroaster, about whom we know very little except that he taught the people to worship one good Spirit, whose symbol was light and fire, and who was always at enmity with an evil spirit, whose symbol was darkness.

The great name connected with the study of the Asiatic branches of the Mother Language is that of Sir William Jones, who founded a society for that purpose and, when he died, left his fine collection of manuscripts, chiefly Sanskrit, to the famous Bodleian Library at Oxford.

Now that we have glanced at these two Asiatic

# BIRTH AND GROWTH OF LANGUAGE 19

languages, let us come nearer home and look briefly at those belonging to the European branch, whose names at least will be more familiar to you.

The first language of which we are going to speak is Greek, the speech of the inhabitants of Greece, who called themselves *Hellenes,* and their language *Hellenic.* We call them *Greeks* from the name given to them by the Romans, *Graeci.* When the first Aryan wanderers (wherever they came from) settled in Greece, they would all be using the same language, but by degrees they would move farther and farther afield and differences of speech would gradually creep in. The natural features of the country would tend to increase these differences, for, as you will see from a map, Greece is divided into sections by alternating valleys and ranges of mountains, and the people of one valley would soon grow out of touch with those in other valleys, for travelling would be difficult and their time would be occupied in tilling the land. As their mode of life changed increasingly with passing years, so their language would develop on different lines in various parts of Greece—the people of one valley would specialise in one branch of industry, and invent or borrow new names for fresh objects and activities; those of another would branch out in another direction; while those near the sea would come in contact with foreign peoples and develop a vocabulary quite different from that of the dwellers in the inland districts.

Thus there grew up in Greece a number of dialects or varieties of the one language, Greek, the three chief being those spoken by the Aeolians, who lived in Asia Minor, Lesbos, Boeotia, and Thessaly, and called *Aeolic*; *Doric*, spoken by the Dorians of Peloponnesus, Crete, Sicily, and Southern Italy; and *Ionic*, spoken by the people of Ionia (Asia Minor), Attica, and many islands of the Aegean Sea.

The Ionian dialect split up again into three—the *Old Ionic* or *Epic*, which is the language of the Homeric poems, the oldest Greek extant literature, before 800 B.C.; the *New Ionic* or the language used by Herodotus, the historian of the fifth century B.C.; and the *Attic* or language of Athens during her most glorious period, 500–300 B.C.

This Attic dialect, though the latest, is the most refined and beautiful form of Greek and lives for us to-day in the writings of Aeschylus, Sophocles and Euripides, of Plato and Aristotle.

The Greeks were pre-eminently thinkers and poets —the greatest philosophers and dramatists that the world has ever known—and to their language we owe many words and ideas used in science, art, and literature of all kinds.

Gradually the Greek Aryans (if we may so call them), who lived westwards, moved farther out in

# BIRTH AND GROWTH OF LANGUAGE 21

that direction and settled in Italy. You will know the legend of the arrival of Aeneas in that country and of his being the ancestor of Julius Caesar.

Just as the language of the settlers in Greece gradually changed so that it differed very largely from that spoken by the early undivided race, so the language of these western wanderers changed still more; so that, although it retained enough of its early character to be recognised as a sister of the Greek tongue, it developed so many new features that it was not always easy to recognise it as a daughter of the Mother Tongue.

When we speak of Greek, we always mean the standard language of Athens at its best; and so, in speaking of Latin, the language of the Latins, one of the peoples of Italy, we mean the dialect which became the most powerful because used by the inhabitants of Rome, who gradually made herself mistress of Italy.

Just as the Aryans seem to have crushed out or absorbed all the former peoples of the countries which they invaded and upon whom they imposed their speech, so it has generally happened that the language of the capital has triumphed over all others. *Greek* means the language of Athens, *Latin* that of Rome. In France, of later times, the dialect spoken in the neighbourhood of Paris became the literary language of the country, owing to the accident that the Capets fixed their capital at Paris, and the same thing happened in England when William I chose London as his capital, and it would seem that in each case that dialect has survived which has absorbed most foreign elements.

Although for beauty and richness Latin cannot be compared with Greek, the former is in a way of more importance to Europe generally because it has become the parent of so many daughter languages, while Greek has given birth to modern Greek only. These Latin descendants are generally called the *Romance Languages*, which we know separately as *Italian, Spanish, Portuguese, French*, and *Roumanian*.

When the Romans conquered a country or a tribe, they left there a colony of Romans, the organisation of which was Roman, the speech Roman, so that the natives had to learn a certain amount of Latin to get on at all. This Latin, however, which gradually mingled with and, in large part, replaced the various native dialects, was not the classical Latin of Cicero and Horace, but the everyday speech of the soldiers, and of the merchants who soon followed when the country had once been opened up. This everyday or *Popular Latin*, as it is called, thus became the speech of all the countries where Rome was mistress, and these daughter languages resemble their mother in varying degrees, as they came into closer or more distant connection with Rome itself.

# BIRTH AND GROWTH OF LANGUAGE 23

Thus Italian is, as we should expect, the Romance language most like Latin; then follow Spanish and Portuguese, Provençal spoken in the south of France, colonised by the Romans and called by them " *The* Province " ; and the farthest off, French.

Italian is, as you know, the language of art, painting, and music—the language of Dante, Boccaccio, and Petrarch ; in Spanish Cervantes wrote the immortal *Don Quixote*; while French had always been the language of chivalry and diplomacy and of such great writers as Molière and Hugo.

But these are not all the European descendants of the Mother Tongue. Some members of the Indo-European race wandered away to the steppes and wilds of Russia, forming thus the *Slavonic* group, which includes besides *Russian*, *Polish*, *Czech* (the language of Bohemia), *Old Prussian* (now dead), and *Lithuanian*, of which we have spoken already.

It would appear that this branch of the family advanced more slowly than the others, for there are a number of culture words shared by the Teutonic languages which do not occur in Slavonic, and we gather also that the Teutons were near the sea and the Slavs were not, for words connected with ships, the sea, and fishing which are common to the Teutonic languages are not found in Slavonic tongues.

Yet another branch of this large family is the

Celtic group, which includes *British*, which survived as Cornish but may now be called " dead," the last person who could speak the dialect having died nearly a hundred years ago.

Another British survival, *Cymric* or Welsh, is better preserved and great efforts have been made of late years to encourage the study of this language by means of a large national gathering, the Eisteddfod, held every year, at which prizes are awarded for the best Welsh poem and for the encouragement of Welsh music and literature and the preservation of the national language and customs.

There are still to be met Welsh peasants who understand little English, and in Wales church services are held every Sunday in Cymric.

A sister speech of Cornish and Welsh is *Breton*, the language of Brittany, and that the two languages have much in common, though separated by the sea, is proved by the fact that the onion-sellers who come over each year from Brittany to Wales can easily understand and be understood in Wales.

*Manx*, or the language of the Isle of Man, is fast dying out, being kept alive only in the speech of the peasants, as is the case with *Gaelic* or Scotch, but *Erse* or Irish is more fortunate, for, as in the case of Welsh, great efforts have been made of late years to preserve the national language of Ireland.

Last, but not least, comes the group to which our

language belongs, the Teutonic, including besides *English*, the *German, Dutch*, and *Scandinavian* tongues.

*German*, or properly speaking *High German*, is of course the language of a large part of Austria as well as of Germany, whereas *Low German* is a name given to the subdivision of this family which includes English, Dutch, and Frisian, the Low German of North Germany.

The Scandinavian group comprises the languages of Norway, Sweden, Denmark, and Iceland, and is interesting as being the language of many of our ancestors, the Vikings, and that in which the old *Sagas* or tales of the northern heroes were written.

Of Gothic, the old language of the Goths, we do not know much, though what we do know is of great importance in the early history of English. The manuscripts of greatest value to philologists are those of Ulphilas, bishop of the Goths, who translated into Gothic probably the whole of the New Testament and portions of the Old, though only parts of his work have been preserved.

## CHAPTER II

### WRITING AND THE ALPHABET

As we asked ourselves in the previous chapter how man first began to speak, we will ask in this " how did man begin to write ? "

You write the letters of the alphabet many times every day; did you ever pause to wonder how it is that by putting twenty-six signs together in every possible combination we can write thousands of words easily understood by everyone who can read ?

Probably not—familiarity breeds inattention, and we are so used to letters and words that we accept them without ever wondering or trying to find out anything about their origin.

Each word we use has a history, so has each letter, and, in the telling of their own story, they often teach us much of the history of their birthplace and the people among whom they first came into being. You cannot study words and writing, or, in fact, anything, without constantly using such words as *book, paper, pen, letter, style, volume,* and the history of these words throws much light on the beginnings of writing.

## WRITING AND THE ALPHABET

*Book* is probably from A.S.[1] *bóc* = a book, also "beech," because the earliest writings were often cut on the bark of this tree, and, in the same way, the Latin word *liber* (from which comes our word "library") means first "the inner bark of a tree," hence "book"; while you probably know that "paper" is from the Egyptian *papyrus*, a reed whose pith was used to write on. The early method of writing was to engrave on waxen tablets, some colouring matter being then smeared into the incised characters; this engraving was done with a steel pen or *stylus*, which gives us our word "style," though the meaning has now passed to the particular character of a person's writing. When you speak of a "volume" you recall, perhaps unconsciously, the fact that in early days manuscripts were rolls of parchment as in Bible times, and we still use the expressions *Rolls of Court, Master of the Rolls, Roll of Honour, roll-call, enrol.*

Have you ever tried to imagine what life would be like without the art of writing? How limited it would be! No communication between friends at a distance, no books, no real literature, no records of the past, no means of ensuring the remembrance of passing events. Truly the pen is mightier than the sword and a powerful civiliser.

In early legend, as among savage tribes to-day,

---

[1] A.S. = Anglo-Saxon.

written signs have always been regarded as a great mystery, of divine origin, allied to magic, black or white as the apparent results seemed ill or good. In the rock inscriptions of Assyria, of which we shall speak later, the king, Sardanapalus V, speaks of the cuneiform or wedge-like signs as being revealed to his ancestors by the god Nebo, and the ancient Egyptians likewise considered the art of writing as a divine revelation.

Among the Chinese the invention of writing was ascribed to the dragon-faced, four-eyed sage Ts'ang Chien, who saw in the stars, in the marking on the tortoise-shell, and in the footprints of birds divinely revealed signs which he used as the foundation of his alphabet.

The Hindoos tell that it was Brahma who taught man to write and that his fingers engraved the marks on the skulls of men, while the old Norsemen believed that it was Odin, the All-Father, who invented the *runes* or characters of the Scandinavian alphabet.

To the primitive mind everything unknown is an object of mystery and fear—the spoken word uttered as curse or blessing has always been accredited with special power; much more then to the ignorant mind are the written characters potent, as may be seen from the wearing of charms and amulets engraved with the divine name to ward off the evil eye, the phylacteries of the Jews, and the passages from the Koran tied round the necks of horses by Mahometans to preserve the animal from harm.

Just as the growth of speech and language must have been very slow, so has it been with the development of writing. From the early drawings of the cave dwellers to the *chefs-d'œuvre* of the writing-masters of the early nineteenth century is a long step, and the ages required for the development must have been many.

The printed letters of our alphabet are about 2,500 years old and we owe them to the Romans, to whom they travelled through various channels as we shall see.

There are, we may say, four stages in the development of writing, though the boundaries of these divisions are not at all distinct; still we may classify them for convenience as follows:

(1) *The Mnemonic* or *memory-aid* stage, when some object is used to give a message or record a fact—of course, not properly writing at all, but a necessary step in its development.

(2) *The Pictorial*, where a picture is drawn to give the message or record the fact.

(3) *The Ideographic*, where the picture is regarded as a sign or symbol.

(4) *The Phonetic*, where the picture or symbol represents a *sound*.

(1) This Mnemonic or memory aid is the most primitive method of communication and record and yet reached a high stage of development among many peoples, and notably among the old natives of Peru, who used a cord to which other cords of various colours and lengths were tied, each colour having a special significance, and each cord being knotted in a different way. One single knot would mean *ten*, two single knots *twenty*, a double knot *a hundred*, and so on, while a green cord might mean *corn*, a yellow *gold*, and, so skilful did the Peruvians grow in the use and reading of these *quipus* or knotted cords, that they kept historical records, and army accounts, and sent orders to the provinces by this means.

Among the Red Indians a somewhat similar use is made of the *wampum belts* made of beads or shells sewn on to fibre, the patterns thus formed indicating tribal accounts, records of victories, treaties, and so on. There are in existence many belts of great historical interest, the one that appeals to us most perhaps being that to be seen in Pennsylvania ; it is called the Penn Wampum, and a well-supported tradition says that it confirmed the treaty between William Penn, the founder of the colony named after him, and the Iroquois Indians (see Plate III).

The belt is made of eighteen strings of white beads, the colour indicating the importance of the agree-

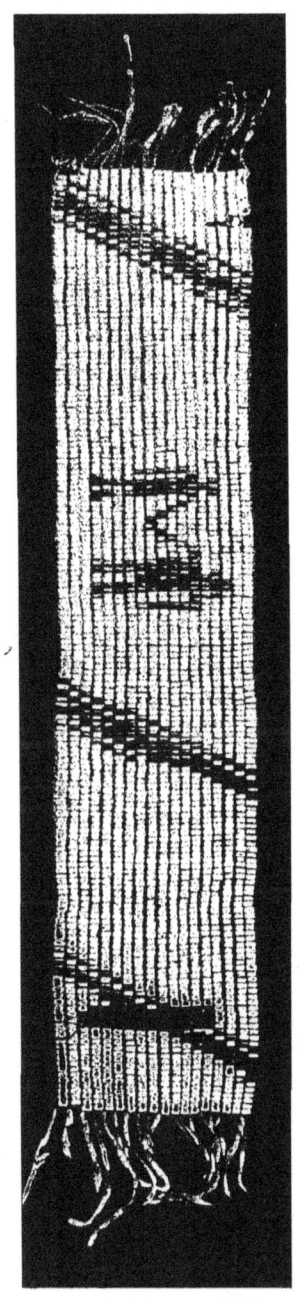

PLATE III.—THE PENN WAMPUM.

## WRITING AND THE ALPHABET

ment; on this background are worked in dark beads the figures of two men; one, evidently an Indian, is holding the hand of the other, whose hat seems to show that he is a European. Across the belt are three oblique lines of dark beads representing rafters, the symbol of the federation of the Iroquois tribes, whose communal dwelling was called the " longhouse."

We have called this method of making records the most primitive, but it is still in use, for do we not knot our handkerchief to remind us of something, do not some people use a rosary, and does not the sailor employ this method when he lets down his logline?

In some countries we find records kept by means of notches made on sticks called *tallies*, and this method of reckoning was in use in England right on into the nineteenth century.

A tally was a squared stick of hazel or willow well seasoned, on which notches of different breadths were cut to indicate the amount in pounds, shillings, and pence which any person lent to the Government, the same amount being cut in Roman figures on the opposite side of the stick. The lender's name and the date were cut on both sides, and the stick was then split in half, one side being kept by the Government, the other by the lender, who, when repayment was required, brought his half, and, if it *tallied* or agreed with that held by the Government, the money was repaid. It may interest you to know that it was the overheating of the stoves to burn the accumulated tally-sticks that caused the burning down of the House of Parliament in 1834.

In former times, too, tradesmen kept their accounts by means of notched sticks, and perhaps you have heard of a *Clog Almanac*. This was a square *clog* or block of wood (or sometimes of other substances) on which were marked the Sundays and Saints' Days, these being indicated by some symbol appropriate to the saint, as a key for S. Peter, a dragon for S. George, and so on.

(2) We now come to *picture writing*, which is still with us in the custom of tattooing and in the trade marks of manufacturers. Among early peoples it was found necessary to mark cattle and movable property to show ownership, and tattooing seems to have been used sometimes so that the members of various tribes might be known apart if taken prisoners in war.

Grave-stones put up by uncivilised races frequently have pictorial inscriptions on them, such as the figure of the totem (or animal specially venerated by a tribe), the hatchet as a symbol of war, the pipe, the symbol of peace; a headless man might represent death, and cutting or weaving instruments might show that the deceased was a woman.

As an example of picture writing we have in Plate IV a reproduction of a petition sent by a group of Indian tribes to the Congress of the United States, asking for the retrocession of lands around some small lakes to the south of Lake Superior.

The *totem* or crest of the leader was a crane, so you will see that the procession is headed by that bird, after that come three martens, representing warriors of the marten clan; another clan is shown by its totem, a bear, and two more by a man-fish and a cat-fish respectively. From the eye and heart of every animal you will see a line connecting them with the eye and heart of the crane to show that all are of one mind, while from the eye of the leader run two lines, one connected with the lakes in question and the other reaching forwards to Congress.

(3) When we pass on to the next stage of writing the characters no longer actually *portray* objects, but *suggest* them; and they do not appeal so easily to the eye, for to understand them some knowledge of the subject or object in question is necessary. For instance, to English people, a picture of two men with clasped hands would suggest friendship or welcome, but to the Chinaman, who clasps his own hands in greeting, the meaning might not be so clear. To anyone knowing something of Christianity, the picture of an anchor, a cross, and a heart suggests

at once the three Christian virtues of faith, hope, and charity, but to a savage or a Mahometan they would convey nothing of this.

Thus the *ideograph* or writing of *ideas*, not objects, is a great step beyond the picture writing, and some of the most interesting ideographs are to be found on the stone monuments and in the manuscripts of the old inhabitants of Mexico.

Some of the monuments are remarkably like those found in Egypt and the inscriptions on some might almost have been taken from the famous Egyptian *Book of the Dead*. The manuscripts are written with a feather pen in bright colours on skins, paper, or cotton cloth, but the key to their full interpretation has yet to be found and comparatively little can be read.

The ideographic stage of writing is well known to us in the form of the pun called a *rebus*, in which a picture stands for the *sound* of the word, as it does frequently in guessing games and in competitions. Thus *Harrogate* would be represented by the picture of a harrow and a gate, and it is this kind of idea-writing that we find among the Mexicans.

In olden days this device was frequently adopted by artists and architects or builders of churches, as you may know from visiting the Islip Chapel in Westminster Abbey, where we find carved in the stone the *rebus* of the abbot who has given his

PLATE IV.—INDIAN PICTOGRAPH.

name to the place—an eye and the slip of a tree held by the hand of a man who is apparently slipping.

(4) The last stage of writing is the *phonetic*, when a sign represents a *sound*, though how the different stages passed into one another we do not know. Still we know that languages tend to become simpler and that economy of effort (or laziness) has always caused difficult and complicated forms to drop; therefore people must gradually have found all other than phonetic forms lengthy and cumbersome, and so gradually evolved this last stage. The Chinese use all kinds of signs, the various forms of pictorial writing as well as signs having a phonetic value, but they have never got rid of the cumbersome and complicated pictorial characters which you have probably seen on tea-chests.

Let us now consider briefly some of the early forms of writing of which we do know something and which in some measure may be said to be far-off ancestors of our own alphabet.

First, and certainly not the least romantic, is the cuneiform or wedge-shaped writing (Lat. *cuneus* = " a wedge ") inscribed on clay or stone in the ancient kingdoms of Assyria (see Plate V).

For many, many centuries these inscriptions were forgotten or unknown, and, even when they were discovered, it was a long time before anyone thought of trying to understand their meaning, if indeed they had any at all.

It was in 1621 that an Italian traveller visited the famous ruined city of Persepolis, the old capital of Persia, and, though he made no attempts to decipher them, he seems to have thought that the wedge-like cuttings on the rocks might have a meaning. He noticed only that the thick end of the arrow-headed signs was always to the left of the sloping characters, and it occurred to him that they had probably been cut from left to right.

High up on a platform, built on purpose in the solid rock, and reached by a splendid staircase, are the ruins of the magnificent palaces of kings long since dead and forgotten. Their bones lie in the tombs cut out in the rock behind and the entrance is guarded by huge figures of winged bulls, such as you can see now in the British Museum. All over the rocks and the walls of these palaces are inscriptions cut out in the cuneiform writing, but for hundreds of years all had stood there silent, deserted, and forgotten, for the secret of the mysterious writing had perished with those who lay buried in the tombs, and the natives of that country-side looked upon these inscriptions with an even greater awe and fear than they felt for the winged monsters that guarded them.

But, though the men who carved the writing were

dead the words themselves were still alive, only waiting the magic touch of learning to wake them that they might disclose the secrets of the past.

After Pietro della Valle, the Italian, a few people made guesses, often very wild and foolish, as to the meaning of the arrow-headed signs, and one man even suggested that not only had they no meaning, but they were merely the traces left by generations of worms!

However, in the eighteenth century some really learned men came to the conclusion that the subject was one worth studying, and Karl Niebuhr, whose father wrote a famous history of Rome, was the first to guess anything of the real meaning of the cuneiform writing. He proved that the characters *were* written from left to right and found that there were three sets of characters, each meaning the same thing, though one was simpler than the other two. He copied some inscriptions very carefully, but could get no farther towards finding out their meaning, and for some time after his death nothing very important was discovered, though scholars thought the inscriptions were written in three different languages, not in three different forms of the same language.

Though many scholars were studying the subject, the real honour of reading the cuneiform inscriptions belongs to an Englishman, Sir Henry Rawlinson, and the story of his work of discovery is full of romance.

He was in the army and was sent to drill the Persian troops, a task which pleased him very much, for he was keenly interested in everything connected with the East and was glad to have the opportunity of making researches for himself. So in 1833 he went to Persia, and, as soon as he was able, he made his way to the rocky platform to copy for himself some of the inscriptions. He climbed the steep face of the rock at great risk, and, although he could not do much at a time, he persevered till he had copied all that was still distinct, and then he found, by patient study, that one of the inscriptions was in a language very like modern Persian, and, when once this was read, it was comparatively easy to read and translate the other two, one of which was in Medic, the language of the Medes of whom we read in the book of Daniel, and the other in Babylonian, a still older language.

Once the cuneiform writing could be read, the history of a whole race of kings and people of whom before we had known very little was found engraved on the rocks and temples and palaces of Persia. These inscriptions were in these languages because the Persians ruled over several conquered nations, as you will know from the Old Testament.

Those who have studied the cuneiform writing tell us that it seems to have started with the pictorial stage, just as other writings did, that the

## WRITING AND THE ALPHABET

arrow-headed lines were cut in clay or on stone to form the picture of what the writer wished to express, but the stiff characters resulting from the use of these straight wedge-like lines soon passed through the ideographic on to the phonetic stage.

If you go to the British Museum, you can see many Babylonian remains and among them a seal which belonged to a king, Sargon I, who lived more than 3,000 years before Christ, and on a tablet near by is inscribed his history; while in the Louvre in Paris are some sculptured panels more than 6,000 years old on which are engraved some vultures hovering over a battlefield and also the description of the fight.

Now it is possible, perhaps probable, that the Egyptians, whose writing we will speak of next, learned their first alphabet from the Chaldeans, who used the cuneiform writing, as we have copies of letters sent to Egypt, written in the wedge-like script—letters about business and the intermarriage of kings and princesses of the two countries, and also copies of the replies from Egypt, and, up to the present, no writing has been found in Egypt that can be dated before the time that the Chaldeans first visited the land of the Pharaohs.

The Egyptians were great artists and loved to make their writing as beautiful as possible, and spent great pains over perfecting it, so that, whereas the Assyrians often scrawled their inscriptions rudely across the surface, with no regard to beauty or regularity, the Egyptian writing is beautifully executed and is a decoration in itself.

As with other forms of writing, that of the Egyptians passed through the successive stages, pictorial, ideographic, and phonetic, though the people were so conservative that they kept the three forms side by side. It is to the great care bestowed by the Egyptians on their dead that we owe the preservation of so much of their beautiful writing, for, apart from the sculptured inscriptions on their huge stone coffins, there are found, buried with the mummies, long extracts from a wonderful religious book, *The Book of the Dead*, copied out on tablets.

Now, the Egyptians were a highly cultured people, and, to express their deep and philosophical ideas, they needed an enormous number of pictographs or ideographs and other signs added to modify or intensify their meaning, and so the matter of writing became exceedingly complicated.

Then at last, one day, we do not know when, there dawned upon man the fact that all the words he used were expressed by the combination of a few sounds. Why not, then, choose from among the huge, confused mass of signs and symbols certain of them to represent permanently certain sounds? When and how this was done we do not know, but

PLATE V—CUNEIFORM INSCRIPTION.

## WRITING AND THE ALPHABET 41

then it was that the alphabet was born, though the first of these phonograms (sound writings) represented *syllables*, not letters, and it was only later that separate signs were used for the different vowels and consonants, and in Hebrew the vowels are not written as distinct letters, but are denoted by distinguishing marks.

The priests of Egypt, who were the learned class, clung to the old form of pictorial writing, but the people welcomed the easier script which seems to have come into daily use about 900 B.C., though, as Alexander the Great (died 323 B.C.) had conquered Egypt, we find later inscriptions in Greek too, a fact to which we owe our ability to read the ancient Egyptian language, as we shall now see.

In the Egyptian room on the ground floor at the British Museum can be seen a slab of black stone that has a romantic history. It is more than two thousand years old and, as you can see, has been worn and scratched by its long sleep in the sands of Egypt. For many years scholars had been trying to decipher the hieroglyphics or picture writing of the Egyptians, but without success. In 1799, when the French under Napoleon had occupied the land of the Nile, a French officer had found this precious slab among some ruins at a place called Rosetta on the delta of the Nile; and, when the English defeated the French in Egypt, the stone was taken over by us and given into the care of Sir William Hamilton, who was keenly interested in such matters. Then for many years scholars gave all their time to trying to discover the secret of the hieroglyphics, and it was found that the inscription was in three languages —the priestly or pictorial characters at the top of the slab, below that the script of the people, while at the bottom the inscription was repeated in Greek (*see Frontispiece*). By comparing the other inscriptions with the Greek, scholars found out the hieroglyphics that stood for the two names *Cleopatra* and *Ptolemy*, which occurred in all three. Shortly after this there was found at Philae, a small island in Egypt, a little monument engraved in a similar manner; and working from the Greek of both, scholars were at length able to decipher the Egyptian hieroglyphics and so read the history of early Egypt.

Can you realise all the time and care and labour that went to the reading of that puzzle ? Think of the secret of that writing being hidden away in the sands of the desert for two thousand years perhaps —silent yet living and waiting to tell us of the ancient King Ptolemy, who lived among the pyramids and the sphinxes and earned the praises of his subjects. For the Rosetta Stone tells of the good deeds of the king: of his lowering the taxes, of his consideration for the priests and the soldiers; of how he built, at his own expense, walls and dams to prevent the Nile flooding the land and destroying the crops. The inscription—which is in the hieroglyphics of the priests, the popular Egyptian writing, and in Greek—goes on to tell how the priests commanded that statues of Ptolemy should be placed in every temple in Egypt, and inscribed with the words, " Ptolemy, the saviour of Egypt," while a copy of the inscription on the slab was to be placed in all the great temples of the land.

Now, we cannot be certain, but it is thought that the Greeks borrowed their alphabet from the Phoenicians, who had simplified one that was used by the people of Crete, who had perhaps taken theirs from the Egyptian hieroglyphics. These Phoenicians were great traders and sailed to many ports of the Mediterranean; and, being a busy, practical people with no time to spare for elaborate and complicated writing such as they found in use in Crete, they made it as short and simple as possible and invented an alphabet—that is, they adopted a number of signs which everyone recognised as representing definite sounds.

You will see that this was a great advance upon the former picture writing, and we have much for which to thank the Phoenicians or whoever it was who invented the first phonetic alphabet, whether it was the direct ancestor of ours or not. We cannot here trace the story of all the descendants of the

Phoenician alphabet, for that would include the study of fourteen Indian alphabets, those of the Hebrew, Arabic, Mongolian, Greek, Russian, and many other languages. We will just mention that it is to the Arabs that we owe our figures, 1, 2, 3, 4, 5, 6, 7, 8, 9, which only slowly came into use to replace the cumbersome Roman numerals, and then we will pass on to the Latin alphabet, which is the one we use, and is, like the Russian, a daughter of one of those used in Greece.

The Latin alphabet is by far the most important of all and was developed gradually from the Greek characters which were introduced into Italy probably about the eighth century B.C. As the Romans conquered other nations they carried with them their alphabet, which soon brought about the disappearance of all others.

No one knows how the order in which the letters follow in the alphabet came about; all we know is that it follows closely that of the Phoenicians, whereas the name is borrowed from the Greek, for we use indeed the first two letters of that alphabet—*alpha, beta.*

It is only since mediaeval times that the letter j has come into use, having arisen from the custom of making the second of two *i's* long, as *ij*; *w* is really two *v's* though we call it as two *u's*, while *y* and *z* were borrowed from Greek by the Latins to represent sounds peculiar to Greek, and you will notice that all English words having a *y* in the body of the word, as *cycle*, are of Greek origin, the *y* representing the Greek *u*, just as our *ph*, pronounced as *f*, represents the Greek letter φ = *phi*.

When you see over a shop " Ye olde curiositie shope " or something similar, the *ye* must be pronounced *the*, for the *y* is really a *th*, for which sound there were two letters in Anglo-Saxon. The one form ð disappeared before 1300, but the other þ lingered on till much later and was gradually confused with *y*, and in old books can be seen the forms *yͤ* and *yͭ* for *the* and *that*.

The Romans of the early empire used two sorts of characters, the *capital* and the *cursive* or running. The first were used for inscriptions and other important work, just as we use capitals now, employing the old Roman forms; the cursive letters were used for letter-writing and other purposes where speed was necessary and were the forerunners of our small type. From this cursive hand there developed a variety of handwritings, the most important being the *uncial* (Lat. *uncia* = " an inch "), so called from the size of the letters. This style of writing was well known to the Irish monks in the sixth century, though who taught them is still a question, unless it was S. Patrick, who may have learnt in Gaul. These Irish monks introduced this writing into Northumbria, and it was the favourite style for all manuscripts down to the end of the twelfth century.

In the King's Library at the British Museum can be seen some beautiful examples of the work of the monks—illuminated manuscripts of all kinds, which are well worth careful study (see Plate VI).

It is to the monasteries of olden times that we owe all our early literature, for none but the monks could write, and but for their devoted labours we should have no text of many valuable and interesting works. In every monastery there was a *Scriptorium* or " writing-room," a large chamber either over the chapter house or in alcoves of the cloisters. Here the monks, whose business and pleasure it was to copy manuscripts, sat each at a desk placed near a window, for the work needed the best light possible, and work was done by daylight only, as candles were dim and grease was liable to be spilt. Each scribe was provided with parchment, ink, pen, knife, ruler, pumice stone for smoothing the parchment, an awl for making guiding lines, a book-rest to hold the book to be copied, and weights to keep the parchment flat and firm.

Absolute silence was the rule of the Scriptorium, and none but the higher grades of monks were allowed to enter. To express needs which were bound sometimes to arise, a code of signs was used, so that if a brother stood up and appeared to be

# WRITING AND THE ALPHABET

turning over the leaves of a book, it was understood that he wanted a book; if he added the sign of the cross then a missal or mass-book was understood. When he wanted a psalter he placed his hands on his head to indicate the crown of David, the psalmist king; and if he needed a daily service book, the monk pretended to wipe away grease that might have fallen from a guttering candle in the chapel.

After settling on the style of writing to be used, the monk planned out his page; then, leaving spaces for all that was to be done in colour, he ruled his lines and began to copy carefully in the most regular of type the text in question—scripture, prayers, legends, poems, chronicles, as the case might be. Though sometimes one monk copied the whole book and illuminated it, as a rule it passed through many hands, and after four pages had been finished the manuscript went to the *rubricator* (Lat. *ruber* = "red"), who added titles, notes, head-lines, etc., in red, or sometimes in red and blue alternately. After this it was the turn of the illuminator, who was allowed to exercise his fancy to the full, so that together with scenes from the Bible and the lives of the saints, appear, in the most beautiful colours, quaint designs, grotesque devices, goblins, demons, and playful fancies, homely scenes, flowers, birds, and strange beasts. Sometimes the portrait of the illuminator himself appears, or that of someone he wished to honour or, occasionally, to caricature. Sometimes at the end of the work the scribe added a remark indicative of his frame of mind—frequently these notes take the form of a pious ejaculation or of pleasure at being honoured with such a task, but occasionally there is breathed in them a sense of relief that the labour is over, and there have been monks who have gone so far as to express a desire for rest and refreshment.

In illuminating, every colour had a special significance, gold and purple were reserved for portraits or the name of Christ; blue and white or a pearly dove-colour were used for the Virgin Mary; red was reserved for Michael the Archangel; Judas was painted black; while for Satan were used the orange and blue of flames and burning brimstone.

When the illuminations were finished, the book was bound, sometimes in thick wooden boards with raised bands at the back, sometimes in more costly bindings of velvet, ivory, embossed leather, gold, or silver. No wonder they were costly, those old books, when so much time and labour went to their making! What tales they could tell if only they could speak!

The style of printing favoured by Caxton and the early printers was called the Black Letter, which was used for all the more popular English books (except poetry and drama) until the early seventeenth cen-

# WRITING AND THE ALPHABET

tury, though the Black Letter is still used largely in Germany.

While talking of the alphabet it may be worth while mentioning the horn-books from which our great-grandfathers learnt to read in the days of the old dame schools. A *horn-book* was not really a book, but a sheet of parchment or vellum about eight inches long by five inches broad, pasted on to a thin piece of wood and its face covered with a thin sheet of horn to keep it clean, the edges often being protected by a metal border. On this small piece of parchment was printed the alphabet in capital and small letters; then followed the numerals from 1 to 9, in Roman and Arabic figures, the Lord's Prayer, and a few syllables (see Plate VII).

At the top of the horn-book stood a large cross forming the first line, which was called the *Christcross* or the *criss-cross row*.

This horn-book, sometimes with a handle like a hand-glass, sometimes without, was tied to the child's wrist or belt by a string and served in turn as reading-book, weapon of defence or attack in juvenile battles, or of chastisement in the hands of the teacher, while it is on record that horn-books were sometimes copied in gingerbread and devoured, as we can imagine, with great gusto. That was certainly eating one's words in a delightful manner!

Shakespeare, in *Love's Labour's Lost*, V. 1, makes

Moth say, "Yes, yes, he teaches boys the hornbook," and Ben Jonson says, "It can be read through the horn," while Dr. Johnson tells us the cross was placed at the top to show that the end of all learning is piety.

In modern days comparatively little time is spent over teaching writing as it was once taught; as soon as a child can form letters independently, it is allowed to develop its own writing largely at will. A glance at any old letters of even fifty or sixty years ago will show, however, that in those days writing was less individual and far more of one type—the fine, pointed style with up and down strokes carefully differentiated—life was less hurried then, and to write delicately was an accomplishment.

The eighteenth century was the age of wonderful writing masters. With a quill pen, with which most of us could make nothing but blots and splutters, the adept would execute the most wonderful designs, flourishes, and letters, large and small, thick or delicate—the great feat being to inscribe as much as possible in the smallest space, as, for instance, the Lord's Prayer in a circle the size of a sixpence. Competitions took place between famous penmen, and great was the pride of the artist who was proclaimed the victor.

Writing of a private school in Bristol in 1782,

Southey says, "One lesson in the morning was all. The rest of the time was given to what was deemed then of more importance—writing. We did copies of capital letters then, and were encouraged to aspire to the ornamental parts of penmanship."

We cannot leave the subject of the alphabet without speaking of the *runes* or sharp angular letters used by the Scandinavians between A.D. 200 and 650. *Run* means in Icelandic "a secret thing or mystery," for, as we have seen, the art of writing has always been looked upon by primitive peoples as mysterious and secret.

It is not certain from whom the Northmen learned their alphabet; some scholars claim it as a daughter of the Phoenician, others of the Latin; a third group consider it a degraded form of the Greek letters, while some have thought that runes were mainly the Latin capitals adapted for the purpose of cutting on wood. Though the runes belong properly to Scandinavia, many runic inscriptions have been found in England, Germany, America, and elsewhere, and strangely enough the runic alphabets, of which there are three—have all been discovered outside Scandinavia.

One of these alphabets or *futhorcs*, as they are called from the first six letters *f, u, th, o, r, c*, is engraved on a knife that was found in the Thames and which can now be seen, in wonderful preservation, in the Saxon room at the British Museum (see Plate VIII), while one of the oldest runic inscriptions was found near Sandwich in Kent. Of the Ruthwell Cross and its famous runic inscription, the *Dream of the Rood*, a poem, we shall speak fully elsewhere in our chapter on English.

The oldest runic inscription known is on a shield buckle now in the Kiel Museum, on which the writing is from right to left and which dates from the fourth or fifth century. Runes seem to have been written originally from left to right like Latin, but they were changed quite early and both methods are found, sometimes mixed apparently as the author liked.

It was not till the sixth century that runes were cut in stone, and after that they were frequently used for inscriptions both on and inside graves.

When the northern people were converted to Christianity the runic alphabet was replaced by the Latin, but in the Gothic alphabet that he is supposed to have devised, Ulphilas preserved, or adapted, certain runes.

One other form of alphabet we might mention is the curious Ogam alphabet, dating possibly from the fifth century and used only in the British Isles. Some scholars think that it is a development of the runes, while others consider it a debased form of the Latin alphabet (see Plate IX).

*Ogam* probably means "skilled use of words," and the letters are formed by straight or slanting strokes drawn above, under, or through horizontal or perpendicular lines.

The greater number of the ogam inscriptions have been found in Ireland, but others are scattered over Scotland, Wales, and the south-west of England.

It is possible, of course, to trace the history of the various letters of the alphabet as they have journeyed to us through the ages, but that would require much time and space, and we have perhaps said enough to show that the whole subject is full of interest and romance and well worth further study.

## CHAPTER III

### ENGLISH IN THE MAKING

IN this chapter we are going to try to answer in some measure a few questions as to the beginnings and growth of our own language—of the words we use so unthinkingly every day.

Why is it that our language is what it is ? how did it grow ? is it wholly and altogether English, and, if not, what other languages have helped in its making ?

When we are young we have an idea that each subject we learn at school is quite unconnected with every other subject; history is history and has nothing to do with geography; arithmetic has no dealings with drawing, and so on; but we soon find out that every branch of learning is closely connected with all others, and so we know that the study of language is intimately related to the study of history, geography, geology, ethnology, and many other subjects.

Even if we had no knowledge of history as a school subject, and knew nothing of the Norman Conquest, with a very slight knowledge of French we could be quite sure that at some time or other the English nation had come into close contact with the French, for every hour of the day we are using words that are quite obviously French—some of them more or less anglicised, others almost unchanged by their passage of the Channel.

As soon as we know even the rudiments of music we must grasp the fact that somehow or other we have had a good deal to do with Italy, for nearly all our musical terms are natives of that country.

The truth is, of course, that English is not one pure language, home-grown entirely and thoroughbred—it is a mixture of many tongues, one to which most of the languages of the world have contributed something. English is indeed a mongrel speech, but is none the worse, and probably much the better, for all that; it is the richest of all tongues, eminently practical, expressive, and the simplest in grammar of all the great languages. (Danish and Cape Dutch are much simpler still, and Chinese has no grammar so far as inflections are concerned.) Our language has been threatened at times by many enemies and has suffered much, but has proved so strong and full of vigour that it has not only survived, but benefited by suffering and has conquered its conquerors, not by driving them out, but by absorbing what was good and useful.

Whereas some languages are rather tied in by

rules and conventions, English is free with the old English love of liberty and elastic enough to admit new and convenient forms and additions which chance throws in its way, though since the days of Shakespeare it has suffered considerable restrictions at the hands of grammarians, schoolmasters, self-constituted stylists, and other pedants.

The foundation of our tongue is, of course, English, the language of the Anglo-Saxons who followed Hengist and Horsa to these islands and drove the poor Britons away into the remote and mountainous parts.

" And did these Britons, or Celts, leave none of their language behind them ? " you may ask. In another chapter you will find their geographical legacy mentioned, so that here we will deal only with their everyday words which remain to us after so many years.

Until lately the number of words generally considered by scholars to be Celtic remains was much larger than it is now, but to-day we can be certain of only half-a-dozen or so, as *bannock* (a cake), *crock* (a jug), *dun* (a colour), *brock* (a badger), *dry*, and *slough*.

While the above are thought to be the only words that we owe directly to the old Britons, we have several other Celtic words which have been borrowed at various times from the Celtic languages—Welsh, Gaelic, Irish, Cornish, and Breton. Some such are :

# ENGLISH IN THE MAKING

Welsh : *coracle* (a tiny boat), *crowd, flannel.*
Gaelic : *clan, loch, ptarmigan, whisky.*
Irish : *lough, shanty.*
Breton : *beak, bourn, budget, car, carpenter, carriage, garter, gravel, vassal, goblet.*

*Bran, clout,* and *gown* are also Celtic.

It is quite natural to find so few Celtic survivals because the men would either be killed or would escape to the mountains with their families, while the women who were captured would become the wives or slaves of the Anglo-Saxons and would gradually learn the language of their captors, though keeping a few terms for everyday objects and household goods, as *bannock, crock, gown, clout* (a patch), *bran.*

When the Anglo-Saxons arrived in Britain they found a people speaking a tongue they did not understand and did not wish to learn, but mixed with this unknown tongue were a few Latin words that had survived from the time when the Romans had lived in this country about a hundred years after the coming of Julius Caesar. Probably the incoming Anglo-Saxons knew a few of these Latin words from their contact with the Romans on the continent, so that they recognised and adopted them and thus passed them on to us. We shall notice the introduction of many Latin words at various periods of English history, but the chief remains of this early period are *castra*, which appears as *chester* and *cester* in place names, *strata* = street, *colonia* = colony, *vallum* = wall, *porta* = port, and *milia* = mile.

The Anglo-Saxons began to arrive in this island about A.D. 455, and, after they had been settled in England for some time, a band of monks under S. Augustine came over the Channel. They were sent as missionaries by Pope Gregory, and as a result of their preaching the various kingdoms of England gradually became Christianised, which change had the effect of civilising and uniting the people so that the union of England under one king became possible; for the Roman priests were great organisers and brought order, and submission to a central authority, where before had been disorder, disunion, and lawless freedom. It was natural that these Roman missionaries, speaking Latin as they did, should teach the English their own names for all church matters, and so we find that many ecclesiastical terms, which are now a part of our language, were introduced at this time and are chiefly Latin by birth; we say "chiefly" because some of them came first from Greece and then travelled to Italy, where they sometimes changed their form a little before passing on.

What travellers some words are and what adventures they have been through since they started on their wanderings! For instance, such words as *ark, altar, candle, chapter, cloister, creed, cross, feast, font, preach, saint, porch, shrine,* all travelled here from Italy in the retinue of S. Augustine and settled down in their new home apparently without much opposition. In a few cases, however, we may trace a slight resentment against this foreign invasion on the part of native words, and for a time two forms, one Anglo-Saxon, the other Latin, are to be found side by side. Thus the English *húsl* was used as well as the Latin *sacrament,* but gradually fell away, though we find the expression *unhouselled* ( = not having received the last sacrament) in Shakespeare. *Húsl-thegn* ( = servant of the sacrament) and *leorn-ung-cniht* (learning-knight) lived on by the side of their Latin equivalent *acolyte* (fr. Gk.) and *disciple.*

Of words which, though originally Greek, came to us through Roman culture a few are *angel, martyr, hymn, psalm, priest, monk, minister, church, bishop, devil.*

But it was not ecclesiastical words only that S. Augustine and his successors brought to England, for to them we owe such words as *box, mint, camel* (Gk.), *cherry, cucumber, lettuce, pepper, sponge* (Gk.), *cheese, pit, chalk, cook,* and many others too numerous to quote, some of them having stayed in France on the way.

It is quite an interesting exercise to take a piece of good English prose or verse and look up the derivation of each word in a dictionary, classifying them according to the language of their birth so that it is possible to find the proportion of foreign words in the language. If you did this, you would find that the percentage of Anglo-Saxon words is about sixty, of Latin and French thirty, of Greek five, the remaining five being taken from various sources.

We have not yet finished with the contribution of Latin to our language, but, to keep to the chronological order of foreign influences, we will leave this branch for a time and look at a few of the words brought over by the Danes.

As we shall see in another chapter, these invaders settled chiefly on the east coast of England, and it is in geographical names that their influence is most clearly seen, but a few of the words we owe to Denmark are *husband, fellow, sky, wing, ugly, want, call, scrub, law, till* (prep.), *take*.

It is quite natural that the English should have adopted many Danish words, for the two peoples were really close relations and had only drifted apart because the Anglo-Saxons came to this country some two centuries before their Danish relatives. The languages of the two were therefore much alike and mingled almost imperceptibly, and it is probable that we should to-day find a greater number of Danish words in our language had not William the Conqueror so ruthlessly laid waste Northumbria where many of the Danes had settled.[1]

Thus the Danes came, saw, and conquered, and were, together with their speech, absorbed by the people they conquered and for a few years this land was free from invasion. Peace, however, did not reign long, for William the Norman had his eye on a country that promised greater scope for his activities than his own dukedom, and so we have the Norman Conquest which had so great an effect on the history of our island. Not only did this conquest change many customs, laws, and manners in England, but it affected the language, though not to such an extent eventually as might have been expected.

The Normans who came over with their duke were mostly nobles who eagerly took all they could get in the way of land and were only too glad to settle down in the new country. Many of them married English wives, they were surrounded by a people speaking English and keeping still to their English customs; and by degrees the nobility lost their distinctive Norman characteristics and became English, proud that their children should be natives of their adopted country.

It is true, of course, that the Normans, like the

---

[1] As it is, a great number of Danish words survived in the more northerly dialects of Middle English and quite a number are still found in the north of England and in the Lowlands.

Danes, were closely related to the Anglo-Saxons, as all belonged to the same stock, but they seem to have changed very greatly during their sojourn in Normandy and to have been regarded by the English as an alien race to a much greater extent than was the case with the Danes.

Even if we had no external evidence of the Norman Conquest, we could, from a study of our language, prove that in every department of life a powerful French influence was exerted on the English tongue at this period.

In connection with the Feudal System, already existing in England but strengthened by the Normans, we find such words as *fief, feudal, vassal, liege* introduced, while the Norman titles *prince, peer, marquis, viscount,* and *baron* first appear and drive out the native *ætheling, thegn,* and *alderman*.

Among military terms that we owe to the Conquest are *armour, siege, lieutenant,* and in the legal world appear *privilege, traitor, justice,* while the Church owes to France such words as *virgin, religion, saint, relic,* all of which words came originally from Latin into French.

If we classify these Romance words and compare them with the English of the period, we find abundant evidence that the French were the rich, the powerful, the refined class, while the English were the peasants, the workers, the homely people, so plainly does language reflect the relations that existed between conquerors and conquered from the death of Harold to the time of the fusion of the two races into one nation.

Note, for example, the names for the animals killed for food—the word denoting the animal alive is English, as *ox, cow, calf, sheep, pig*, while the name for the flesh to be eaten is French, *beef, veal, mutton, pork*, a fact easily explained when we remember that the peasants rarely tasted meat, which was an ordinary article of food among the richer Normans. The humbler *breakfast*, too, is English; the more sumptuous meals of *dinner, supper, feast,* and *banquet* are French.

Names of trades and professions are largely Romance in origin, for the English had not been a nation of traders or scholars; so we find that the humble *weaver, baker, ploughman,* and *miller* are native, while the *grocer, butcher, tailor, painter,* and *joiner* are foreign, that is Romance, together with art words, as *colour, beauty, design,* and terms such as *fashion, apparel, costume, dress,* while *clothe* is Teutonic.

Still, though a number of Romance words crept into our language during this period, the main fabric of our tongue *is* English, and we may wonder perhaps how it was that the English people, unlettered as they were on the whole, learnt any French at all.

The truth is that they did not learn much—their everyday speech remained much as it was, and still is almost purely Teutonic, but they learnt a little French in two ways. They quickly picked up French words that were like their native English, as Fr. *neveu* (nephew), A.S. *nefa*; Fr. *riche* (rich), A.S. *rice*; and there grew up besides among the more learned classes the habit of using the French word side by side with its English synonym, in writing if not in conversation, and many examples of this usage can be found in early literature.

For instance in the *Ancrene Riwle* we read: " Charitie (R.) that is love (A.S.)," while Chaucer says: " Thereto he could endyte (R. = write) and make (A.S. = compose) a thing ( = poem), Swinken (A.S. = toil) with his hands and laboure (R.)."

In the Prayer Book we find many examples of these Teutonic and Romance doublets, as " we acknowledge (A.S.) and confess (R.) "; " I pray (R.) and beseech (A.S.) you "; " dissemble (R.) and cloke (A.S.) "; " assemble (R.) and meet together " (A.S.) all of which examples are taken from one passage, namely, the Exhortation at the beginning of the Morning Prayer.

Sometimes one or other of the doublets was dropped, but very often both have been kept, the native word retaining a more homely meaning, the Romance term showing its connection with the higher

PLATE VI—AN ILLUMINATED MANUSCRIPT OF THE FIFTEENTH CENTURY.

walks of life. Such are the English *bloom, buy, feeling, luck, work, friendly, hut, clothe* as compared with the Romance synonyms *flower, purchase, sentiment, fortune, labour, cordial* (or *amicable*), *cottage,* and *dress*.

It is to the adoption of these foreign synonyms in addition to, and not in place of, the native words that the English language owes its richness and suitability for expressing fine shades of meaning.

French influence on English was considerably increased by the Hundred Years War begun by Edward III, and you will know how largely Chaucer was indebted to France in his earlier writings, both for subject matter and treatment. But the rise of the English national consciousness caused the native element to assert itself, with the result that we have the *Canterbury Tales* and Wycliffe's translation of the Bible in the London dialect which was taking its place as the standard language and which received the badge of superiority when Caxton introduced printing into England and chose that form to perpetuate. This rise of a national consciousness caused the English writers to keep the native word side by side with its French or Latin synonym, as we have shown above, so that the English word lived on in the language of literature as well as in the speech of the people.

Synonyms are very useful for avoiding repetition

and for expressing slight differences of meaning, for it very seldom happens that they have retained quite the same meaning during the years they have existed together. As examples of this we might take the work *ask* and its synonyms *beg, entreat, beseech, implore, pray, request, appeal, demand.*

*Ask* is English and has the meaning of wishing to obtain what may reasonably be expected, as *I asked for a ticket.*

*Beg* is Romance and has the idea of appealing to pity or sentiment, usually to a superior, or for politeness to an equal, as *She begged me to overlook the offence* ; and *I beg your pardon.*

*Entreat* (Lat.) means to ask repeatedly and earnestly—*I entreat you to save the child.*

*Beseech* (Eng.) = to ask reverently and humbly —*We beseech Thee to hear us, good Lord!*

*Implore* (Lat.) = to ask with emotion—*She implored forgiveness.*

*Pray* (Lat.) = to ask of God—*Let us pray.*

*Request* (Lat.) = to ask formally—*Your company is requested.*

*Appeal* (Lat.) = to call upon the sympathy —*We appeal to you for help.*

*Demand* (Lat.) = to ask peremptorily—*They demanded my passport.*

At the end of the fifteenth century the *Renais-*

sance, or *Revival of Learning* in Europe generally, caused the introduction of many new words into England. We need not here go into all the causes of this revival, but may just remark that it was largely due to the flight of learned men from Constantinople on the advance of the Turks. These scholars carried with them to Italy, where most of them fled at first, many classical manuscripts which had up till then been unknown to Western Europe and the study of which opened up a new world of literature to the scholars of many countries.

This revival of learning was helped considerably by the invention of printing, which had taken place some years before, and by the spirit of inquiry and the love of adventure and liberty encouraged by the discoveries of Columbus and others, and by the desire for greater liberty in the realms of thought and religion which caused men to think and study for themselves instead of being content to believe and act as others told them.

For the many new ideas that were born at this time new names had to be found, and instinctively scholars went back to the language of learning during the Middle Ages—Latin; while the religious discussions of the time brought us into conflict with Rome, and till the Reformation Latin was the language of the whole Church, as it was of the law.

In some cases certainly borrowing from the newly

learnt Greek took place, but it was to Latin that we owed most at this period. In many instances Latin roots from which words had been formed in previous days we now used again; though you will see from the examples below that the later reborrowing differs somewhat in meaning from, and is much more like the original than, the earlier derivative, which is what we should expect, as the first word came to us through the French and was adopted by the people as a whole, whereas the second was formed by scholars directly from the Latin. Modern science still borrows from Greek and Latin and forms names for new inventions, and advertisers do the same, as in *telegraph* (Gk.), *telephone* (Gk.), *gramophone* (Gk.), *pneumatic* (Gk.), *bovril* (Lat.), *sanatogen* (Gk. and Lat.).

| *Latin* | *Early Borrowing through French* | *Later Scholarly Derivative* |
|---|---|---|
| balsamum | balm | balsam |
| captivus | caitiff | captive [1] |
| fragilis | frail | fragile [1] |
| potio | poison | potion (through Fr.) |
| traditio | treason | tradition [1] |
| poenitentia | penance | penitence [1] |
| pauper | poor | pauper |

and from Greek we have:

| | | |
|---|---|---|
| blasphemein | blame | blaspheme [1] |
| skandalon | slander | scandal |
| phantasia | fancy | phantasy [1] |
| kalux | chalice | calyx |

[1] Probably through French.

## ENGLISH IN THE MAKING 69

As the *Revival of Learning* took place first in Italy, scholars from all other European countries flocked thither to study the precious manuscripts rescued from Constantinople; and when they returned to their own country they took with them many Italian words and expressions; and all through the Tudor period Italy exercised a strong influence on the language and literature of England. Chaucer had borrowed largely from Italy both for ideas and style, and the Elizabethan writers followed his example, as you will know from the number of Shakespearean plays in which the scene is laid in Italy. It is the same with all other writers of the period, and it is to Italy that we owe the sonnet.

Added to this we have the fact that at the beginning of the sixteenth century Genoa and Venice were the great maritime and commercial powers of the Mediterranean; and the Italians were deservedly famous for their art, music, and manufactures, and passed on to other nations words connected with these subjects.

From Italian we have among many others such words as *alto, contralto, soprano, cantata, oratorio, pianoforte, sonata,* and the art terms, *studio, vermilion, fresco, cameo* and *bust,* while among general words we have *volcano, umbrella, regatta, macaroni, influenza, carnival.*

You will remember that it was the Spaniards and Portuguese who first led the way in the geographical discoveries of the fifteenth and sixteenth centuries, and that there was long and keen antagonism between Spain and England, in spite of, and one might almost say partly as the result of, the marriage of Queen Mary to Philip II of Spain. This close connection with Spain caused the introduction of many Spanish words into England at this period, some of which are *cargo* and *chocolate*, a word which the Spaniards borrowed from the Mexicans whom they conquered.

*Cochineal, cork,* and *cigar* are also Spanish, together with *banana, anchovy, cockroach, rusk,* and *battledore,* which should really be *batedor,* a flat piece of wood with a handle used for beating clothes in washing (cf. Fr. *battre* = "to beat").

Some words originally Spanish came to us through the French, as *cannonade, ambuscade,* and *barricade,* which really means " a protection formed by barrels filled with earth."

About the time our language absorbed these Spanish words we borrowed also some from the Portuguese, such as *albatross, veranda,* and *fetish* from the Portuguese word *fetico,* " sorcery," literally " artificial," applied to the idols which they found among the native tribes of Africa. The *coco-nut* was so called by the Portuguese from the monkey-face at the base of the nut, the Portuguese and

# ENGLISH IN THE MAKING 71

Spanish word *coco* meaning "a bogy," or "ugly mask to frighten children." The *binnacle*, in which a ship's compass is kept, should really be *bittacle* from the Portuguese *bitacola* meaning "a chest or bin"; the word being a shortened form of the Latin *habitaculum*, "a little habitation," hence "the frame of wood on a ship where the compass stands."

You will know from history that during the seventeenth century England and Holland were struggling for the rule of the sea which the Dutch had gradually gained on the decline of Venice, Genoa, and Spain. During this struggle, in which the Dutch finally lost, the English language took over from the enemy a number of words, many of them nautical terms, as *ahoy, reef, skipper, stoker, yacht, hold, boom, hull, hoist, deck, cruise, bowsprit*. During the wars in the Low Countries in the reign of Elizabeth, and from the merchants who came to London, we learned the words *beleaguer, blunderbuss, knapsack, trigger, wagon, brandy, ledger*.

The Dutch painters of this period were deservedly famous and their connection with England gave us such words as *easel, landscape, stipple*, while other Dutch words found in England are *wainscot, hop, guelder-rose, frolic, fumble*, and *hottentot*, and the more modern borrowings as *trek* and *boer* which date from the South African War.

Of pure German words there are not many examples

in English; both languages sprang from the same stock and are still in vocabulary somewhat alike. Some of the few words we have borrowed are *swindler, waltz, zinc, plunder,* and *poodle*.

*Landau* comes to us from a town of that name in Bavaria, while *cobalt* should really be spelt *kobold,* the name for a demon, the German miners having given it that name because they considered it very poisonous. The *meerschaum* used for the bowls of pipes really means " seafoam," and both compounds appear in English as *mere* (a lake) and *scum*.

Carlyle was very fond of the literature and language of Germany and did much to make them better known in England, making frequent use of the Teutonic form of hyphened adjective common in Old English; as in *amber-locked, thunder-voiced, snow-and-rosebloom maiden, god-announcing oracle,* while other writers have introduced, upon the German model, *standpoint, folk-lore, fatherland*.

We said earlier in this chapter that there are few languages in the world which have not contributed to make English what it is to-day, and, amongst others, Turkey has given us *ottoman, caviare, kiosk;* Hungary has given us *coach,* Poland *polka* and *mazurka,* Russia *steppe, cossack, mammoth,* and *tundra,* though few of these are *direct* borrowings.

The languages of Asia have done their part and given us *calico, chintz, sepoy, shampoo, jungle* from

# ENGLISH IN THE MAKING 73

India, *caddy*, *satin*, *tea*, and *mandarin* from China, while from the Malay Peninsula we have *gong*, *gutta-percha*, *sago*, *cockatoo*, and *bamboo*, from Arabia *sherbet*.

From Hebrew we have taken *cherub*, *alleluia*, *seraph*, *jug*, and *log*.

Words have travelled to us also from darkest Africa, from America and Australia, for the Congo gives us *zebra*, and Egypt gives us *sack*, *satchel*, *paper*, *oasis*, *ammonia*, though none of these words has come to us direct, but all have passed through some other country, as Italy, Greece, or France, to get to us.

The kaffirs of South Africa have supplied us with *quagga* and *gum*, Morocco has sent us *morocco* and *fez*, while from the West Coast we have *chimpanzee*, *guinea*, *gorilla*, *yam*.

Across the sea from the New World have travelled *toboggan*, *tomahawk*, *wigwam*, *squaw*, and *moccasin*; Mexico sends us *jalap* and *tomato*, and Hayti names for us *mahogany*, *maize*, *potato*, and *tobacco*. If you are in a *canoe* during a *hurricane*, you can think of the West Indies, the home of those words; *tapioca* should remind us of Brazil, while *quinine* and *alpaca* should carry our thoughts to Peru.

Though the natives of Australia are few and low down in the scale of civilisation, they have given us such words as *kangaroo* and *boomerang*, while the many islands of the South Seas have sent us *taboo* and *tattoo*.

We do not, of course, pretend to have given more than a few examples of the many foreign words that have taken their place side by side with the native words in our language, but we have said enough to show how greatly we are indebted to other nations for their share in the making of English and we must confess that our language has been greatly enriched by these contributions.

We might certainly have coined new names for all the fresh ideas and objects that have continually come to us, but that was not worth while when we had only to take those that offered themselves full of the romance of the East, the mystery of ancient Egypt, or the adventures of the New World.

## CHAPTER IV

### THE GROWTH OF ENGLISH

WE have seen that, though many tongues have helped to make the English language what it is to-day, the main body of our speech is native. But in the course of centuries this English has suffered many changes, and in a page of Old English or Anglo-Saxon, such as that written by King Alfred, the greater number of words would wear a different dress from that they wear to-day, even if their features were recognisable.

We all like to hear about the childhood of our friends, so let us look a little at the childhood and growth of our own language and trace its development into the speech we use to-day.

You will know that most languages, Greek, Latin, and German, for instance, are highly inflected—that is, words suffer change of form to express difference of case, gender, number, tense, degree. Now, though modern English makes very little use of inflections, Old English was a highly inflected language—nouns varied in form to show difference of case, and there were many declensions; adjectives were also declined and agreed with their nouns, and gender was a matter of grammar, as in modern German, and not one of common sense decided by sex as in modern English.

We will not go into these Old English inflections in detail, but will mention only those that have remained until now or have had some influence on the English of later times.

If Old English was highly inflected and Modern English is scarcely inflected at all, why, when, and how did these inflections disappear?

Let us first answer the question *when?* and we shall have to say that no one can give an exact date, for the process was gradual. Our forefathers did not meet together one day in council and decide that thenceforth they would drop all, or nearly all, inflections and start fresh with a simplified language.

The change came gradually and unnoticed by most people, so that it was only by looking back many years and comparing the language of their own day with that spoken by their forefathers that they could see that changes had come about.

Though no definite boundaries can be set to the various periods of English, it is usual to consider them roughly as follows:

(1) *Old English, Early English, or Anglo-Saxon* are terms which embrace many dialects known under

the general name of English. This period of full inflections lasted from early literary times till about 1150, our last Old English document belonging to the year 1154.

(2) *Middle English*, the period of fewer inflections, 1150-1450, during which the language gradually changed from the "analytic" to the "synthetic" form. There was still no standard English language proper, but only a number of varying dialects. (From the Conquest to the last part of the fourteenth century French was the official language. It is from the London dialect used by Chaucer that our standard English is descended.)

(3) *Modern English*, the period when all but a very few inflections were dropped. It was the introduction of printing by Caxton that caused the dialect of London to attain pre-eminence and form the basis of standard English.

In dealing with languages as regards the grammatical relationships of words, we divide them into two classes, *synthetic* and *analytic*, as mentioned just above. A language which, as Greek, Latin, or Anglo-Saxon, expresses the grammatical relationships of words in a sentence by means of inflection (case and tense endings, etc.), is called *synthetic*, from two Greek words meaning "put together," while a language which, as modern English and French, uses prepositions and auxiliary verbs instead of inflections is called *analytic*, from two Greek words meaning " loose."

In synthetic languages the order of words in a sentence is not of such great importance as it is in those which are analytic, for in the former the subject and object of the sentence are almost always clearly differentiated by case endings, so that there can be no doubt as to the meaning. In Modern English, however, where no special ending marks the objective case, it is most important that a definite word-order should be recognised, in order to avoid confusion.

If, for instance, you say in Latin *Venator leonem occidit*, the style might be affected, but not the sense, by changing the order of the words; whereas, if you wrote in English " The hunter killed the lion," and then transposed it thus, " The lion killed the hunter," it would make all the difference to the sense—and to the hunter !

Although in Old English the word-order was not quite so regular as it is in Modern English, it was still a matter of greater importance grammatically than it is in Latin. The inflections disappeared long before a regular word-order was developed, which fact makes the understanding of Middle English often a matter of great difficulty.

All languages exhibit this tendency to drop inflections, but English has gone farther than any other,

# THE GROWTH OF ENGLISH

and it is to this fact that we owe the great use we make of prepositions and auxiliary verbs to express the many shades of difference in meaning which make our language so rich and so expressive.

It used to be thought that this decay of inflections was a loss, and that the farther a nation advanced in civilisation, the more complex would its language become, but, as a matter of fact, we find that it is the primitive peoples that have a complex speech, and that all languages tend to become simpler, and this simplification is now regarded as a gain rather than a loss.

From this point of view, then, English is the most advanced and the most enlightened of all languages and therefore the most suitable for expressing the wants and thoughts of man.

The questions "how and why" the whole nature of the English language has changed we will answer together. If, as we have suggested, English is one of the most advanced of all languages, why is it so? Is it because we, as a nation, have always been much cleverer and more enlightened than other peoples, so that we have deliberately evolved a perfect and simple speech for ourselves?

We cannot say that English is perfect as a language, nor can we claim any merit, for, as a matter of fact, the whole thing came about quite naturally and considerably against our will as a nation, seeing that the two events that tended most to the simplification of English were the Danish Invasion and the Norman Conquest, and neither superiority of intellect nor education had anything to do with it. If the matter had been left to the cultured class, the language would probably have changed much less than it did, for this class is always the most conservative in such matters; it is the uneducated masses that bring about changes in speech, and that, as we shall see, is what happened in England.

All the time that our tongue was changing so much, the languages of the other nations of Europe were changing too, but, owing to successive inroads of foreigners into England, our language suffered, or perhaps we should say benefited, more than others.

The first part of Anglo-Saxon England to develop a literary language was Northumbria, the home of Bede, but the coming of the Danes quenched the lamp of learning in the North and the conquering Danes settled down among the conquered Angles. These two peoples, however, were closely related and their languages very much alike, so that each could understand the speech of the other; so it came about that these two tongues, Danish and Anglian, mingled, and, because they were *spoken*, not *written*, in the mingling many of the grammatical inflections were confused, forgotten, and dropped.

The three chief dialects of Early English were

# THE GROWTH OF ENGLISH 81

Northumbrian, Midland or Mercian, and Southern or West Saxon, and of these, as we have seen, Northumbrian was the first to develop any literary importance. Of this early Northumbrian literature very few specimens remain, but one of them is the poem called *The Dream of the Rood*, which has a romantic history.

In the parish of Ruthwell, in Dumfries, is an ancient cross, which is thought to have been set up about the year 680 (see Plate X). It is adorned with scenes from the Gospels and with inscriptions which, for many years, no one could read. For long ages it stood in the church, but in 1642 it was broken down, and during the next hundred years was used as a seat. Then it was moved to the manse garden, the fragments were put together with all possible care, and in 1840 John Kemble, the historian, read and translated the inscription. It was found to be in runes and to record about forty lines of a poem on the Rood (the Cross), written in the Northumbrian dialect.

But this was not all.

Some time after this discovery, an Anglo-Saxon manuscript was found in the north of Italy, at Vercelli, which was one of the regular stations on the old high road to Rome, used by all the northern people. In this Vercelli book were found verses in the dialect of Wessex, which verses proved to be a translation of the Northumbrian poem, " The Dream of the Rood."

On the top stone of the Ruthwell Cross is this inscription in runes : " Cædmon made me," *made* here probably meaning " wrote," or " composed," so that the author of the poem may have been Cædmon.

The Danish invasion, which affected the Northumbrian dialect so largely, had less influence on that spoken in the Midlands, and scarcely any on that of Wessex, which continued for a long time, fully inflected. This is the language of almost all the Early English or Anglo-Saxon literature we possess.

In this language are written the poems of *Beowulf, Widsith* (The Far Traveller), *The Battle of Maldon, The Seafarer,* the spirited *Anglo-Saxon Chronicle,* containing our early history and the story of Alfred's fights with the Danes, and the fine prose of Ælfric and Alfred.

Just as the Northumbrian dialect lives on to-day in the speech of Lowland Scotland, in the poems of Burns, in the dialects of Yorkshire and in the northern hills and dales, so traces of the language of Alfred can be heard in the speech of the western counties even now. Unaided by books and unencouraged by education, these dialects have shown a wonderful vitality which has enabled them to endure through many changes and to be active and living to-day.

# THE GROWTH OF ENGLISH

So entirely was West Saxon the predominant language of early England, that, had it not been for the Norman Conquest, we might now be speaking a Low German tongue, something like modern Dutch, to which family, you will remember, English belongs.

William of Normandy did come, however, and West Saxon was no longer the language of the educated and literary class, but of the peasants, so that, unchecked by the conservative influence of the learned, English changed very quickly. The mass of the people could not write at all, and pronounced, or mispronounced, words as the unlettered still do everywhere, and these mispronunciations were passed on from generation to generation till the correct forms were entirely forgotten.

As was natural, the endings of words would be slurred over or clipped in speaking and then omitted altogether, so that the case-endings of nouns and adjectives were gradually weakened to *e*, or to *es* or *s* for the plural or possessive. The various inflections of verbs showing difference of person were also levelled, just as they are to-day by uneducated people, when they say, " I done it," " we done it " ; " I says," " we says."

What was more, those of the people who did write, wrote as they spoke, and spelt entirely according to sound ; not knowing much of grammar, they used as few inflections as possible, and, to make up for these, used prepositions and auxiliary verbs freely.

No one can say exactly when particular grammatical changes took place—when, for instance, the noun plural *as* became *es*, or the infinitive ending *an, ian*, changed to *en*, or the past participle prefix *ge* was dropped, and when *to* began to be used before the infinitive. All we can say definitely is that the change took place gradually; during a period of transition, generally about a hundred years, both forms were used side by side, and the most that we can say is that a certain form is not found in any known manuscript before or after a certain date and so get a rough idea of the process of simplification.

But the Norman Conquest had another effect on our language, for the indirect result was that the East Midland dialect, that spoken round about Cambridge, became the standard English, in place of that spoken in Wessex.

This change was largely due to the fact that, with the coming of the Normans, London, situated on the borders of the Midland district, became the capital in place of the Old English capital Winchester, which was in Wessex; and the language of the capital would naturally be largely used for trade and intercourse with the continent. Besides this reason, the two universities of Oxford and Cambridge

## THE GROWTH OF ENGLISH 85

were in the Midland district and it was natural that the most learned men of the times should gather there and talk and write in the language of the district. Later came Chaucer and Wycliffe, both speaking and writing a dialect mainly Mercian and perpetuating it in their works; and after them came Caxton, who printed the works of Chaucer and further helped to standardise this form of English.

So it comes about that we inherit the bulk of our language from the Midlands. Less Danish than that of Northumbria and less inflected than that of Wessex, it was understood by the borderers of each and afforded a half-way house between the two, borrowing forms from each and incorporating them in its own.

Some Northern forms adopted by the Midland dialect were *are* in place of the southern *sindon* (cf. Mod. Ger. *sind*); *they, them, their*, and *till*; while *some* replaced the southern *thilke*, which survives as *ilk, of that ilk*, though its modern users generally ignore the fact that it was in A.S. a pronoun, meaning " same," always used with the definite article, for they seem to regard it as a noun meaning " kind " or " class." [1]

---

[1] If any noun is implied as following *ilk*, it is *place*, for the O.E. word *ylca* was used when the name of the landowner and that of his family estate were identical—as in " Rasay of that ilk," i.e. of Rasay (Johnson's *Journal of a Tour in the Hebrides*).

As we have said before, the language of the Anglo-Saxon invaders of this country and that of the Danes were originally so similar that, when the latter settled in England, the two peoples had little difficulty in understanding one another and their languages melted almost imperceptibly into one.

But you may ask, " Seeing that the Anglo-Saxons died long since and left us no gramophone records, how do we know how Old English was pronounced ? "

A complete answer would be long and complicated, but we may say briefly that an idea of the pronunciation can be gained from a careful study of kindred languages still spoken. At Oxford there is an interesting manuscript, dating probably from the tenth century, and giving certain Greek texts in Anglo-Saxon characters which clearly reproduce, not the original letters, but the *sounds.* As Greek at that time was probably pronounced almost, if not quite, as it is to-day, by comparing the letters by which the Anglo-Saxon scribe transliterated the Greek sounds we have direct evidence of the values he assigned to the Old English letters themselves.

The Scandinavian, or Danish, invasion was really a source of wealth to our language, for words which were already English were often adopted again with a slight difference of meaning, so that we have such forms as *house* A.S. but *husband* Sc. ; *drop* A.S., but *drip* Sc., though the forms are really identical.

## THE GROWTH OF ENGLISH 87

Similarly we find *ride* and *road* A.S., but *raid* Sc.; *slay* A.S. but *slaughter* Sc.; *sit* A.S., *seat* Sc., and many others.

Sometimes we have the *sound* of a word from the southern dialect, and the *sense* from the northern, as in the case of the word *dream*, which is, in sound, the A.S. *drēam*, M.E. *dreem*, meaning not *dream* at all, but *joy, happiness*; whereas the northern word *draumr* means just *dream*.

Speaking of this rise of the Mercian dialect in the place of that of Wessex, Professor Skeat says, " It is a curious reflection that, if London had been built on the south side of the river, the speech of the British Empire and of the greater part of North America would probably have been very different from what it is now."

Still, things having happened as they did, and the loss of inflections having proceeded with increasing rapidity during the later Middle English period, we find that, the spelling being then approximately fixed by printing, the English of Elizabeth's time looks very like that of to-day, though we notice that Shakespeare uses many old forms and expressions that are not now considered grammatical.

The bulk of Shakespeare, however, would to-day be quite intelligible to a silent reader of very little learning, whereas Chaucer, in the original spelling, would, even with the help of a glossary, present considerable difficulty and the language of the earlier writers would appear a foreign tongue.

English, since the days of Shakespeare, has changed chiefly in respect to pronunciation and a greater strictness in the matter of grammatical forms; and a standard of correct English gradually came to be set up from which no educated person can differ.

The century following the Renaissance was one of enterprise and invention in the realm of language, of licence and extravagance; and Shakespeare and his contemporaries could use almost any part of speech as any other part; they could use a plural verb with a singular subject and *vice versa*; could employ such forms as " most unkindest," " *in*charitable," " *in*fortunate," " *un*proper," and yet in the main their English is to the eye that of our day.

The chief difference between the English of Elizabeth and that of the present time is, as we have foreshadowed above, in the pronunciation. We will not here discuss the changes which most of our vowel sounds have undergone since the sixteenth century, but it would be hardly too much to say that if a company of actors were to play Shakespeare with the exact pronunciation of his day, we should, most of us, understand very little that was said. You can test this for yourself by reading rhymed passages from Shakespeare or any other writer of his time, and even of the time of Dryden and Pope, and you will notice that words are used as rhymes then which, with our modern pronunciation, would be quite out of court.

In *Richard II* occur the lines :

> "He does me double wrong,
> That wounds me with the flatteries of his tongue,"

while you probably remember the pun in *Julius Cæsar*, which runs :

> "Now is it Rome indeed and room enough,"

the words "Rome" and "room" being pronounced alike in Shakespeare's time.

In Dryden we read :

> "For present joys are more to flesh and blood
> Than a dull prospect of a distant good,"
> ("The Hind and the Panther")

and again :

> "They durst not rail, perhaps; they laughed at least,
> And turned them out of office with a jest."
> ("Epistle to Henry Higden, Esq.")

Pope writes :

> "At once they gratify their scent and taste,
> And frequent cups prolong the rich repast."
> ("The Rape of the Lock")

and :

> "On rifted rocks, the dragon's late abodes,
> The green reed trembles, and the bulrush nods."
> ("Messiah")

The Authorised Version of the Bible has exercised considerable influence on the English language, setting, as it does, an example of simple and dignified prose, full of poetry and music, and yet able to be understood by the least educated. Fortunately for us, and probably for English style in general, the translators of 1611 kept very closely indeed to the beautiful version of the earlier translators, instead of recasting it in the involved and heavy Latinised style in fashion at their day—the style of Hooker, for instance; and you have only to read the terrible language of the dedication to King James at the beginning of the Authorised Version, and compare it with the language of the Bible itself, to be heartily thankful that we were preserved from a translation of the Bible in a style so heavy and wooden.

Had the translators not used so simple and stately a style, it is safe to say that the Authorised Version would not have exercised the influence on English literature that it has, nor would its contents have become household words as they have.

Modern English has become almost entirely analytical; it has been further enriched by a number of new borrowings from many sources, and by the coining of many new tokens for scientific discoveries and inventions, and by a greater licence in the formation of compound words to express new ideas.

We have seen that English has changed from a

# THE GROWTH OF ENGLISH 91

synthetic to an analytic language, but it has changed also in another direction. Whereas Early English was a *pure* language—that is, it contained in the main words of native origin only—it very soon began to absorb words from other tongues, so that we now find only about 60 per cent. of the words in our language are really English by birth.

Such being the case, it may be of interest to note what classes of words are essentially English or Teutonic, such are:

All nouns forming their plural by vowel change, as *foot, feet*.

Almost all nouns with singular and plural alike, as *deer*.

All pronouns.

All demonstrative and distributive adjectives.

All numerals except *dozen, million, billion*, etc.

All adjectives of irregular comparison, as *bad*.

All auxiliary and defective verbs.

Nearly all strong verbs.

All weak verbs, excepting *catch*, that have different vowels in the present and past tenses.

Almost all prepositions and conjunctions.

Most of the adverbs of time and place.

You will find that it is quite easy to make sentences on ordinary subjects without using a word of Latin or French birth; but it is very difficult to make even the shortest English sentence by using only French or Latin words, and you will notice that when we adopt foreign words we nearly always make them conform to our grammatical rules.

The chief influence that French has had on our language, apart from its gift of actual words, of which we have spoken in another chapter, is to be seen in the matters of word-building and spelling. Many of the prefixes and suffixes still used for forming new words are of Romance origin. The French feminine suffix *ess* took the place of the English *ster*, other French suffixes being *ace* (populace), *ade* (cockade), *age* (courage), and many more; while of the numerous prefixes we may mention *ad* (advice), *re* (render), *bene* (benefit).

The chief, perhaps the only, harm that French did to our language was to upset the phonetic spelling that marked it in its early stage. In the thirteenth and fourteenth centuries the English tongue was respelt according to the Anglo-French method by scribes who knew Anglo-French but not Anglo-Saxon. Still, though they did not know Early English, these scribes knew, studied, and, in fact, saved for us, Middle English, and by the fourteenth century many of the earlier inconsistencies of spelling of the previous century were corrected.

It is to French influence that we owe the compound *qu* (the sound of which had been represented in Anglo-Saxon by *cw*), the *s* sound of *c* before *e* and

# THE GROWTH OF ENGLISH 93

*i*, the sound of *g* as *j* before the same vowels and the letter *i* used as a consonant to denote the sound now expressed by *j*; so that almost all words containing the letter *j* are of French birth.

Our present chaotic spelling is largely due to the fact that so many sounds (especially vowel sounds) have been lost in the course of centuries, and others have arisen for which we have no separate symbols, with the result that one can seldom tell from the look of a word what its pronunciation may be.

Caxton spelt phonetically in the main; but, with the Renaissance, scholars tried to show in the spelling of a word something of its origin, and, as the zeal of these early scholars was often greater than their knowledge of etymology, words were frequently misspelt.

For example, the words *sythe* and *sent* were respelt *scythe* and *scent*, just because the word *science* began with *sc*. But the last was a strictly classical word from Lat. *scio*, "I know," whereas *scythe* is from A.S. *siðe* (a cutter) and *scent* from Lat. *sentire* or Fr. *sentir*.

Just so the M.E. *ake* (from A.S. *ac-an*) was rewritten *ache* because it was thought to be connected with Gk. *achos*. *Rhyme* should be *rime* (A.S. *rim*), but was confused with *rhythm* (Gk.), just as *style* should be *stile*. The good old Anglo-Saxon word *tunge* or *tonge* was respelt *tongue*, to look like the French *langue* and the Latin *lingua*; for, unfortunately, these well-intentioned people knew something of Greek and Latin, but nothing of Anglo-Saxon, and so our spelling suffered severely at their hands.

The spelling of English has changed little since Tudor days, but, as we have said, the pronunciation, especially of the vowel sounds, has altered considerably—hence the difficulties and anomalies of English spelling and the consequent suggestions for reform.

As Professor Skeat says, " Practically we retain a Tudor system of spelling with a Victorian pronunciation."

When we use the expression " Modern English " we mean what is frequently called " good English," or the language of the educated class spoken all over the country, untouched by any peculiarities of intonation or phrasing which might show from which class or district the speaker came.

The origin was, as we have seen, probably the Court English and the language of the upper classes of London in the fourteenth century; it was not a pure dialect, but an admixture of the English of the South and the Midlands with a sprinkling of Northern words.

The Southern dialect was spoken in London till the twelfth century, after which the Mercian gradually replaced it, being very likely considered at first just the then fashionable way of speaking, but soon becoming the accepted form of correct English everywhere.

You must remember that no one form of English is intrinsically better than any other; superiority is entirely a matter of greater suitability for the expression of ideas.

A dialect may be, and in some cases probably is, a much better form of language to express the ideas and needs of those who use it naturally than that accepted and used by the majority, and any one dialect can attain to a position of superiority only from the fact that that majority consider it so much more useful and expressive than any other that it becomes the aim of all to acquire it.

What we now call Standard English happens to be the dialect that was selected by the more educated class of the later Middle Ages as that best suited to the expression of their ideas and so has reached its pre-eminent position, but had circumstances been other than they were the choice might have fallen equally well on either the Northern or the Southern dialect.

It is a mistake therefore to think that because some people persist in calling Standard English *good* English, provincial or vulgar (i.e. of the people) English must be *bad*. As forms of language the various provincial dialects may be as good as Standard English, and to the philologist and historian at any rate are as interesting and important as the one that has been standardised. You will find, moreover, that in many points it is all a matter of chance or fashion, for many words and expressions once considered " vulgar " are now a regular part of the standard language, while others which once enjoyed that position are now cast out by the elect. Much that is considered vulgar to-day is so only by convention and just because the polite dialect has chosen to put its hall-mark on another form; and a large number of so-called vulgarisms are historically as correct as the expressions received by the majority. Thus, for example, the provincial pronunciation of such words as *boil, join, oil,* namely *bile, jine, ile,* which is heard too in Oxfordshire and Berks as well as in Ireland, is historically correct, as you will see from so late and so classical a writer as Pope, who uses such perfectly good (in his day) rhymes as " line " and " join." Most of the critics who have charged Dryden and Pope with using bad rhymes have had no knowledge of English phonology, and therefore have had to put up a claim for " poetic licence " on behalf of poets who, if anyone did, kept the classic rules.

We all know many points in which Standard English differs from the dialects either in matters of pronunciation or choice of words and phrases, but it

PLATE VII—A HORN-BOOK.

# THE GROWTH OF ENGLISH

may not strike you at once that Standard English itself is also a variable quantity. Even among the speech of the most educated there are variations due to fashion, individuality, or regional causes.

Thus most people in the North and Midlands pronounce the *a* in *dance, bath,* more like the *a* in *fat,* while the Southern generally uses a sound like the *a* in *father.* Some again pronounce the vowel sound in words like *halter, salt, cost, cough* something like *aw,* while others use the vowel sound of *not* in these words and yet say *awffice* (office), *mawth* (moth).

Some people reverse these pronunciations while others mix them, and yet both forms are accepted.

It is on record that the same person may use two pronunciations of the same words to mark difference of meaning, as, when he speaks of the animal, he says *ass* (with *a* as in *fat*), whereas in applying that epithet to another person he says emphatically *ass* (as in *father*), though others would just reverse the process saying *ass* (*father*) in mentioning the animal, and *ass* (*fat*) in derision.

Of changes due to fashion we may mention the once popular *'erb* (*herb*), *'ospital* (*hospital*), and the individual peculiarity of sounding the *t* in such words as *apostle, epistle.*

The pronunciations *Derby* and *clerk* (as *Turk*) are historically quite correct, but the sounds *Darby* and *clark* have so completely usurped their place that they only are now accepted among the educated.

But English has changed since the days of Elizabeth not only in the matter of pronunciation, but also, as we have just mentioned above, in greater restriction of grammatical freedom, whether for good or ill each must decide as he thinks.

It may be of interest to note here some instances where the accepted Elizabethan usage differed from that now generally considered correct, and you have only to turn to the works of Shakespeare or any of his contemporaries to gather any number of examples for yourself.

The Elizabethans claimed much greater freedom in the matter of case usage of pronouns, frequently using the nominative when we should use the objective and *vice versa*.

For example we read in *The Merchant of Venice*, III. 2, 321:

"All debts are cleared between you and *I*"

in *Antony and Cleopatra*, III. 3, 14 :

"Is she as tall as *me* ?"

and in *Othello*, IV. 2, 3:

"Yes, you have seen Cassio and *she* together."

Again, *us* is used often for *we*, as in :

"Shall's to the Capitol ? "
(*Coriolanus*, IV. 6, 148.)

and *thee* for *thou* after the verb " to be," as :

" I would not be thee, nuncle "
(*King Lear*, I. 4, 204.)

a usage which has almost received sanction in Standard English of modern times in the colloquial " It's *me*."

Relics of the dative case are to be noted in the use of *me* and *him* without a preposition (explained in annotated editions as *ethic dative*) in places where we should say the pronoun was in the objective case after a preposition understood. Such are :

" He plucked *me* ope his doublet " (me = for me = for my benefit)
(*Julius Caesar*, I. 2, 270.)

We find also *he* used for *man*, and *she* for *woman*, as in :

" Lady, you are the cruellest *she* alive."
(*Twelfth Night*, I. 5, 259.)

" I'll bring mine action on the proudest *he*
That stops my way to Padua."
(*Taming of the Shrew*, III. 2, 236.)

Another frequent Elizabethan usage is the omission of the relative as in *Measure for Measure*, V. 2, 23, where we read:

> "I have a brother (who) is condemned to die,"

and in *The Winter's Tale*, V. 1, 23:

> "You are one of those
> (Who) Would have him live again?"

We often find a singular verb following a relative that is plural, as in:

> "'Tis not the many oaths *that makes* the truth"
> (*King John*, II. 1, 216.)

and in *Cymbeline*, I. 6, 117:

> "'Tis your graces that charms."

In the case of verbs the falling off of the past participle ending *en* often causes the Elizabethan writers to use the shortened form common in early English, so that we find such forms as:

> "Have you *chose* this man?"
> (*Coriolanus*, II. 3, 163.)

Sometimes, if they feared the confusion of this curtailed participle with the infinitive, they used the past tense for the past participle, as in:

> "When I have *took* them up"
> (*Julius Caesar*, II. 1, 56.)

# THE GROWTH OF ENGLISH 101

Many irregularities are found also, as:

> "You have swam"
> (*As You Like It*, IV. 1, 38.)

and:

> "I have spake"
> (*Henry VIII*, II. 4, 153.)

A practice of the Elizabethans that has been followed by Carlyle is the formation of adjective compounds in which the first adjective acts, to some extent, the part of an adverb.

In *Richard III*, III. 1, 44, we find the line:

> "You are too senseless-obstinate, my lord,"

and in *Julius Caesar*, I. 3, 124, we read "honourable-dangerous."

After the passing of the Elizabethan era, we have, with Milton, the end of the Romantic and the beginning of the Classical period. The Civil War did something no doubt towards the spread of the now generally accepted Standard dialect, and the Augustan Age of Dryden, Pope, and Johnson drew the free structure of English more closely together; this probably being partly due to the rigid rules of the French classical school of the period under the influence of the Academy, founded by Cardinal Richelieu in 1635.

The discipline of this period may have been good for English literature and probably cut off pernicious growths that had sprung up after the passing of the Elizabethan masters, but it is doubtful if many to-day (outside Cranford) care to read the English of Johnson.

You cannot really fetter a language; English has had many enemies who would bind her with chains of iron and reduce her to a lifeless machine, but, like a human being full of individuality and life, she has broken the bonds of convention and developed in her own particular and sometimes wayward manner, and long may she continue so to do!

If, as we have seen, our language has changed so materially since the days of our Anglo-Saxon forefathers, how much or how little remains to us of the grammatical forms of their times? With the object of finding an answer to this question, let us look at a few words with a little more attention than is usually accorded them, for surely they deserve it after so long a life and such varied experiences.

Words are like travellers from a far country, wandering among many peoples, staying here, passing quickly there; sometimes treated with respect and welcomed, at others ill-treated, robbed, and mutilated. Yet, outliving all the people among whom they

# THE GROWTH OF ENGLISH 103

wander, they are with us to-day, as full as ever of life and vigour and reproductive force; occasionally unchanged after all their adventures, but generally altered or disguised by their travels through the realms of time.

Let us look first at a few nouns that have resisted all efforts, both of time and man, to deprive them of their own distinctive case-endings, so that to-day, like heroic standard-bearers, the survivors of many fights, they proudly flaunt their rescued possession before the eyes of men.

In Anglo-Saxon, though *es* was a frequent ending of the genitive (or possessive) case, its place was often taken by *e*, or *an*, and a good example of these alternatives is shown in the names of the days of the week that we write so often. *Tuesday*, *Wednesday*, and *Thursday* have still the genitival *s* because the names of Tiw, Woden, and Thor, the gods who gave their names to those days respectively, formed their genitive by adding *es* (the *e* has since disappeared); but Freya and the sun and moon, to whom the other three days were dedicated, took *u* or *an* in the genitive, endings which have proved less enduring than the hissing *s* sound, which, you will find, is always the last to disappear.

The name *Saturday* had two forms in Old English —*Sætern-daeg*, which was simply a compound and required no sign of the genitive, a case appearing in the form *Sæternes-daeg*, which fell out of use as being less easy to pronounce.

You will notice, as a point of interest, that this last day of the week is the only one whose name is of Latin, not Teutonic origin.

By the fourteenth century *es* had become the only genitival ending for singular and plural, though for some time it continued to be sounded as a separate syllable, as you will see by reading Chaucer aloud, and even Shakespeare uses it thus occasionally, as in *A Midsummer Night's Dream*, when he writes, " Larger than the moonës sphere."

When we now write *'s* for the possessive, as *boy's*, *girl's*, the apostrophe represents the lost *e* just as it does in French when we write *j'ai* for *je ai*.

Of the old dative endings we have few examples left among our nouns, for this ending consisted usually of *e, a, an,* or *um,* and fell more easily than the genitival *s,* for it was more easily slurred and swallowed in pronunciation. This old ending *e,* however, is still preserved in the word *stone,* where the *e* was once a separate syllable, the nominative being *stān*; while *meadow* and *shadow* are both descended from the dative and not the nominative which had no *w*.

If Modern English had descended chiefly from the Southern instead of from the Midland dialect, it is probable that our plural ending would be *en* instead of *s*. Both these forms and others existed, but the *es* and *s* again proved the stronger, so that we have only *oxen* remaining of the other type, though Shakespeare writes *shoon* for " shoes," and we find *hosen* (hose) in the book of Daniel; all Londoners know Clerk*en*well, where the *en* is the plural ending, while *housen* (houses) can still be heard in the south of England, though in Anglo-Saxon the plural of *hūs* (house) was *hūs*, the same as the singular.

Except in the case of a few learned words, such as *agendum*, pl. *agenda*, *stratum*, *strata*, all borrowed words have had to submit to this method of forming the plural, so that the Greek *bishop*, the Latin *lion*, the Italian *solo*, and the French *gewgaw* all form their plural by adding *s*. In the case of a small number of borrowed words we have kept the foreign plural in addition to that formed in England, each then having a slightly different meaning, as in the case of *cherub*, *cherubs*, *cherubim*.

You will no doubt think that *children* and *brethren* are examples of the old plural ending *en*, and so they are, but they deserve a remark all to themselves, for they have the distinction of being plural twice over. The *r*, which in both these words precedes the *en*, was a sign of the plural, but was followed by a vowel; when this vowel fell off, people, forgetting that the *r* was itself a sign of the plural, added *en* to make it correct, as they thought.

As for the nouns, like *deer* and *sheep*, which have

the same form for singular and plural, they remained unchanged in Early English, and formerly there were many other words like them, as *year, head, folk, pound, horse, night, score*, which fact explains our use of such terms as *twenty head of cattle*; a *body of* 1,000 *horse*; *ten score*; *a fort*(fourteen)*night*, our forefathers reckoning by nights instead of days, just as they reckoned years by winters.

In Anglo-Saxon, adjectives were fully declined and agreed with their nouns, but their case-endings, too, were gradually levelled to *e* (pronounced separately as in Chaucer's "grēnë grass"), and then finally dropped. The only remains of these adjectival case-endings are in *olden*, where the *en* seems to be the weakened survival of *an*, and in *these* and *those*, which were both originally the plural of *that*.

It is, of course, quite illogical of us to change *this* and *that* for the plural, when we do nothing of the kind with *his, her, our, my*.

Of the adjectives of quantity we may notice that *little* (A.S. *lyt, lytel*) has really no connection with its comparative *less*. The original of *lyt* was *lytig*, "deceitful" from *luton*, "to betray," so that *little* still sometimes means "base, mean, small-minded."

*Half* is A.S. *healf* = "side," so that "on your behalf" means "on your side, in your interests."

In the expression "the more the merrier," the *the* must be traced back to the old instrumental case, a sort of ablative, so that the expression really means "by what degree more, by that degree merrier"; while the final *t* in *that* is a sign of the neuter gender (cf. *it, what*, both neuters), but before the end of the Middle English period, *that* could be used in any case and for any gender and number.

Our comparative and superlative endings *er, est*, are from A.S. *ra, ast, ost, est*, and you will notice that Shakespeare often compares adjectives by adding these suffixes, where we should now prefix *more, most*, as, for example, when he writes "ancienter," "honourablest," and you will find that Carlyle follows the Elizabethans in this. *Other, either, whether, after, under, further*, are all really comparatives, while *lesser* and *nearer* are doubly so, for *less* is the comparative of *little*, and *near* the real comparative of *nigh*.

*Rather* is really the comparative of the old adjective *rathe* = "early," and is used in poetry, Milton saying in *Lycidas*:

"Bring the rathe primrose that forsaken dies."

The writers of the Tudor period often used double comparatives and superlatives, such as Shakespeare's "more kinder," "more sweeter," and in *King Lear* we have:

"Let not my worser spirits tempt me again."

In the Authorised Version we read, "After the most straitest sect of our religion I have lived a Pharisee."

The pronouns retain several of the old case-endings, as the *r* of *our*, *your*, *their*, and the *n* of *mine* and *thine*, which are relics of the old genitive, and this *n* still lingers in the language of the unlettered, who say *hisn*, *ourn*, *yourn*.

The *m* of *him*, *them*, and *whom* is a legacy from the old dative case, though now we say these words are in the objective case.

The pronoun *its* is quite modern and was not used at all in England till 1598, when it occurs in Florio's translation of Montaigne's *Essays*; and, indeed, it occurs very seldom after that till Dryden used it constantly. We do not find it in the Authorised Version of the Bible, where *his* is used instead, as in "Put up again thy sword into his place"; Milton uses it three times, Bacon very seldom, and it occurs in none of Shakespeare's plays published in the author's lifetime.

English children are often puzzled to know why *its* should be written without an apostrophe, but the reason is that the apostrophe represents an omitted *e*, and such a form as *ites* never existed, so that no apostrophe is needed.

You may be surprised to hear that Ben Jonson did not recognise *who* as a relative, but only as an interrogative, for he speaks of " our one relative

# THE GROWTH OF ENGLISH 109

'which.'" Elizabethans in general used *who* and *which* quite indiscriminately, as in the Bible we read " Our Father, which art in heaven "; " God, who at sundry times, etc."

Shakespeare also says " a lion who roared " and " It was the owl . . . which gives the stern'st good night."

An Anglo-Saxon verb had really only two tenses, present and past, though a future could be formed with *shall* and *will*; the subjunctive mood was used frequently, especially in indirect narrative, and the participles were fully declined as adjectives.

The infinitive ended in *an, ian,* and had a dative case preceded by *to*; the endings *an, ian,* were weakened later to *en* as in Chaucer, and this suffix is still used to form verbs from adjectives, as *ripen, deepen, sweeten, blacken, straighten,* etc.

*To* is used very frequently in Old English before the infinitive (inflected), and for this *to* we often find *for to* in Middle English, as *for to go*; and the A.S. ending *en* for the three persons plural was retained till the end of the reign of Henry VIII, and Ben Jonson laments its loss, which made singular and plural alike.

The ending *eth* of third person singular fell during the middle English period, and was replaced by *s*, though the *eth* is still found in the Authorised Version of the Bible, in the reading aloud of which, too, you will notice that the *ed* of the past is still pronounced as a separate syllable, as "He giveth his belovëd sleep."

You know that the past tenses of many Greek and of some Latin verbs are formed by reduplication—that is, by repeating the root syllable—and a few Anglo-Saxon verbs did the same, though most of these reduplicated forms have been lost. *Dread* was originally one of these verbs, the old past being *dreord*, where the *rd* at the end was a repetition in inverse order of the *dr* at the beginning, the letters having changed places by a process called *metathesis* or "change of position," which caused A.S. *grapse* to become M.E. *grasp*, and A.S. *wapse* to become *wasp*.

In Anglo-Saxon *fell* and *held* were reduplicating pasts, but the repeated syllable has fallen and the only real example we have left (and that is used only in poetry) is *hight* = "named," which was originally *he-hait*.

It is a great pity that the present participial ending *end* (Midland), *inde* (South), *and* (North) fell out of use, to be replaced at the end of the twelfth century by *ing*, for this change has led to much confusion between the various classes of words ending in *ing*. The old forms still lived on and were used by some Elizabethan writers when they wished to write in an old-fashioned style; Spenser uses "glitterend" and Ben Jonson speaks of "trilland

# THE GROWTH OF ENGLISH 111

brooks," but the *ing* was fairly well established by 1350.

The Anglo-Saxon past participle of most verbs could be preceded by *ge*, sounded more like *ye*, and it is this prefix, written *y*, which Spenser used frequently.

In the opening lines of *The Faerie Queene* we read,

> "A gentle knight was pricking on the plaine,
> Ycladd in mightie armes and silver shielde."

This prefix survives now only in the old poetic form of "called," *yclept*.

Several of the auxiliary verbs have undergone a slight change of meaning since early days. Thus *can* originally implied not merely ability as now, but knowledge and skill, just as *können* does in Modern German. Its adjectival form *uncouth*, which now means "clumsy," "unrefined," meant "unknown." In this adjectival form we have an indication of the correct spelling of "could," which has taken to itself an *l* to be like "should" and "would." The analogy is, however, faulty, for the last two words get their *l* from "shall" and "will," whereas "can," from present tense *con* or *can*, has none.

The early form of *may* (*mæg*) was used where we should now use *can*, and for the idea of possibility sometimes expressed by *may*, the Anglo-Saxons had a form *mot, moste*, our *must*.

*Ought* is the past tense of *to owe* and had the meaning of being in debt; and though now the only auxiliary which takes " to " before the following infinitive, it was used by Shakespeare without it, as in " you ought not walk."

The two words *do* in " how do you do ? " are not the same word really; the first is the verb " do " used as an auxiliary of interrogation, but the second is from *dugan,* " to avail," which survives in this one expression only.

*Shall* was seldom used as a simple auxiliary in old English, its early meaning being " to owe," from a much earlier form *skila,* " to kill or wound," *skall,* " I have killed or wounded," therefore " I am liable to pay the wergeld or life money." In Modern German *Schuld* means both " guilt " and " debt," and Chaucer used " shall " in this old sense when he said, " For by the faith I shal to God " = " I owe to God," and we keep this old meaning of obligation in mind when we say " Thou shalt not kill," " He shall do it."

In Anglo-Saxon there were two verbs, *willan,* " to will," and *wilnian,* " to desire," and the resemblance of form and meaning caused these verbs to be confused and the form *wilnian,* " to desire," has quite died out. *Willan* had a negative form *nyllan* = " not to be willing," which has survived in the expression " willy-nilly " = " will he nill he " = " whether he will or won't."

# THE GROWTH OF ENGLISH

Adverbs are especially interesting, for all were originally some case of a declinable word—noun, adjective, or pronoun.

In Early and Middle English the genitival suffix *es* was used to form adverbs from nouns and adjectives, so that we have *summeres* (in the summer), *winteres, daies* (by day), *willes* (of his own will = willingly), *other whiles* (at some other time). Although *niht* (night), being feminine, did not take *s* in the genitive, an adverb *nihtes* was formed on the analogy of *daies*, and we still have the expressions "o' nights," "a or o' Sundays," "now-a-days."

Most of these forms have long since disappeared, but the genitival *s* remains (though sometimes written *ce*) in *else, hence, since, once, always, sometimes, backwards*.

This adverbial *s* lived on into the sixteenth and seventeenth centuries, for Shakespeare says in *The Merry Wives of Windsor*:

"Come a little nearer this ways"

and in the Prayer Book we read "anyways afflicted or distressed," while we still say sometimes "it's early days yet."

In Old English, adverbs were sometimes formed by the use of the dative ending *um*, which lives on now as *om* in "seldom" and the old-fashioned "whilom," A.S. *hwilum*, at times.

"At random," which you might think belonged to this dative class, is from French *à randon* = "in great haste."

Examples of adverbs formed from the objective case of adjectives and nouns are *somewhat, yesterday, meantime, half-way, enough, north, south, east,* and *west.*

Our modern adverbial suffix *ly* is the descendant of the A.S. *lic* = "like," while the adverbs, such as *hard, fast,* which have the same form as the adjective, had originally an adverbial suffix *e* which quickly fell, leaving them as they are now.

There are a few adverbs which have given birth to verbs in rather a strange way, such being *sideling* (or *long*), *darkling, grovelling* ( = flat on the ground). The suffix *ling* or *long* is A.S. adverbial ending, and looks so much like a present participle ending that verbs have actually been manufactured to go with the supposed present participle which was really an adverb. Thus we can now say "to grovel on the ground" (where the meaning of the verb is repeated), "to sidle up to a person," while Thackeray uses "to darkle."

Our prepositions were originally adverbs which modified verbs, as "they came *near*," serving thus to show more clearly the verbal action. As time went on, they forsook the verb and became attached to nouns, helping the disappearance of case-endings and taking to themselves the office they now hold.

# THE GROWTH OF ENGLISH

Now, of course, all prepositions are said to govern the objective case, but in Anglo-Saxon they governed the genitive and dative as well.

All our prepositions are of Teutonic origin, except a few modern borrowings occasionally met with, such as *per, versus, maugre*. *Over, after, near, under*, are comparative forms; the *a* in *abreast, once a day, across*, is a shortened form of *on*, and the *o'* in *o'clock* is really *of*. The phrase *to and fro* preserves for us the Middle English form of "from," *fra* or *fro*, while *among* is from A.S *on mang*, literally " in a mixture or crowd."

Conjunctions are of late growth and have sprung from other parts of speech, especially pronouns, adjectives, adverbs, and prepositions, or compounds of these, many being in fact the same as the adverb and preposition, but used in a different sense and relation.

Thus we have very briefly seen in outline the growth of our native tongue and its development from a pure, synthetic language to one that is the most analytic of all tongues and certainly not pure.

We have elsewhere claimed that words are *alive*, and this brief glance at the growth of English has surely shown us that languages, as people, are affected by circumstances, surroundings, and the people they meet. And, as people change, so does language.

English, though generally speaking grown-up and settled, is still growing and developing. New words are constantly being borrowed from other tongues or coined to meet some new want; from the forcible and often picturesque language of slang fresh words often pass into the standard speech, while other words, which denote objects no longer in use, tend to pass away.

And our mother tongue is living and begetting daughters, if we may so name the varieties of English which are springing up everywhere in our colonies, especially perhaps in North America, Australia, and New Zealand.

So, with a life like the ebb and flow of the sea, language is ever moving, rolling through the centuries, bearing in its heart a message from the past ages for all who care to read.

## CHAPTER V

### SOME ANOMALIES IN ENGLISH

"Every word we use comes to us coloured from all its adventures in history, every phase of which has made at least a faint alteration."

So says a modern writer,[1] and it is our intention to follow in this chapter the adventures of some of our everyday words.

The changes and adventures of some words can be traced and classified, while the history of others is partly or wholly unknown, but everywhere we must notice the wonderful vitality of words—their power to live and retain some signs of their parentage after all the ill-treatment they have undergone at the hands of man during their age-long existence.

Just as we say sometimes of people that they have gone up or come down in the world, so we could say with equal truth of words; as people lose a limb, or perhaps two, so do words; as men replace a lost limb by an artificial one, so can words adopt a sound in place of one they have lost; and as a man uses

---

[1] G. K. Chesterton, *Blake*.

a stick though he has two legs, and an eyeglass though he has two eyes, so words have sometimes developed a second form while the first still exists.

The first of these changes, a rise in the world, is to be seen in a word like " fond," which originally meant foolish and still has that meaning in the north of England. Shakespeare and other writers before and after him use it in that sense, and though we generally understand it to mean " affectionate," we still keep the old meaning in the expression " fond hopes."

A "shrewd" person once meant one who was malicious, from an old English verb meaning " to curse," which idea is kept in the old expression " beshrew me ! " With us a " minister " is either a high government official or a clergyman, but the word originally meant nothing more than "servant"; and " nice," that much-abused adjective, first signified " fastidious," while " gentle, generous, ingenuous," now used of moral qualities, were once applied to birth and position.

A sacrament to us is a solemn service, but to the Roman soldier it was the oath that he took to his general; a martyr was just a Greek witness, and any messenger was an angel, while paradise was just a royal park.

A steward was once the sty-ward or keeper, just as a marshal was the horse (mare) servant, while

Christian, Quaker, Methodist, once terms of reproach, are that no longer.

Just, however, as we probably know more people who have come down in the world rather than gone up, so we find that more words have changed their meaning for the worse than for the better.

For instance, no one now would care to be called a knave because we understand it to mean "rogue," whereas it originally meant simply a serving-boy; just as "churl" meant a man, a simple freeman of the lowest rank. "Libel," now a legal offence, really means "a little book," and "villain" is the modern spelling of *vilein*, a peasant, and has nothing to do with wickedness.

No serious poet of to-day would dream of calling the Muses "imps," as Spenser did in his *Faerie Queene*:

"Ye sacred imps that on Parnasso dwell."

Again, in Hall's *Chronicle of Henry VIII* we read "that his sonne Prince Edward, that goodly imp, may long reign over you," and the epitaph of Lord Denbigh in Beauchamp Chapel, Warwick, runs thus: "Here resteth the body of the noble impe Robert of Dudley, sonne of Robert, Erle of Leycester"; which quotations show that "imp" was once used quite seriously meaning "son," "offspring," "scion," from its original meaning "a graft on a tree," from the Sanskrit word "to be," so that it is one of the words having a very long life-story.

"Silly" originally meant "timely," then "happy, blessed, lucky, innocent," and is simply the English form of the German *selig*, "blessed," and has assumed its present meaning in modern times. The "sexton" who digs graves was in olden times the "sacristan" who kept the sacred vestments, and in connection with this word an amusing story is told by the Rev. S. Baring Gould in his book *The Parish Clerk*, which, whether strictly true or not, illustrates the way words change in pronunciation and meaning on the tongues of the unlettered.

A visitor to a church is asking the old man who shows him over if he is the verger, and the old man replies to this effect. "Well, the first vicar he calls me clerk, the next he calls me beetle (beadle), the next he calls me virgin (verger), the next he calls me Christian (sacristan), and now I be virgin again."

Nowadays no one would care to be called a gossip, but its early meaning was "godmother" or "godfather"—a relation in God, from O.E. *sib*, "a relation," which word is in turn descended from a Sanskrit word meaning "fit for an assembly," therefore "trusty."

It is often quite impossible to explain how it is that words have lost their original dignified meaning and taken to themselves one that is often almost comic.

Who would now speak of his head as his "pate" or "noddle" except in joking? Yet "pate" is to be found in the Prayer Book version of the Psalms, "his wickedness shall fall on his own pate," and "noddle" occurs in a poem of Hawes.

The following expressions, now anything but dignified, are to be found in the various early editions of the Bible. "Barnabas and Paul rent their clothes and skipped out among the people" (Wycliffe). "The Lord trounced Sisera and all his host" (1551); and Tyndale speaks of "a sight (= a multitude) of angels." Milton, in speaking of Christ's travelling through the air at His temptation, uses the expression "His aery jaunt," and in another place says "to save one's bacon," while a translator of Livy (Holland) says that the Romans were "in the dumps" after their defeat at Cannae.

"Crafty" (which in German means "strong") originally meant "skilful," as did "cunning"; "huzzy" was simply "housewife," while the modern use of "awful," "terrible," "fearful," as a synonym for "very" is seen in the expressions "awfully jolly," "fearfully funny," "terribly late."

There is another class of words which have changed their meaning with the passage of time, those which now have a wider application than formerly.

One such is "triumph," which now means any victory or success, but originally meant the honour of a triumphal procession which was granted to a victorious Roman general.

A "privilege" was in times past "a law passed relating to any one person," but now means "any right enjoyed by one or many over others." An "idea" really means "the look or appearance of a thing," not a "thought," as it does now; and "influence" was always used of the power of the stars over human affairs. "Legion" is now used to denote any great number, whereas it really means a select band of Roman soldiers, from 4,200 to 6,000 men; and when we say the population of a country was "decimated" by disease or famine, we are misusing the expression employed by the old Romans to explain that every tenth man (Lat. *decem* = "ten") was chosen for death or punishment.

When you hear some one say "What a preposterous idea!" he is really saying, "That idea is hind-part before," though he thinks he is saying, "What an extraordinary and impossible idea!" A butcher is now one who sells any kind of meat, whereas originally he killed and sold only goats, the word "butcher" coming from an old French word *bochier* = "one who kills goats"; O.F. *boc*, Mod. Fr. *bouc*, "a goat."

There are, on the other hand, words which have

become specialised or narrowed in meaning, as "acre," which once meant any ordinary field and now means 4 roods. "A furlong" or "furrow-long," was the usual length of a furrow, that is about 220 yards long, the length found by experience to be the most convenient distance for a team of oxen to plough without stopping. So a rod, pole, or perch, which we take as 5½ yards, was really the length of a pole used by the ploughman in Anglo-Saxon England to urge on his oxen.

"Yard" really means a "rod" or "stick," as the yard arms of a ship's mast, and, of course, is quite a different word from "yard" of which "garden" is only another form. "Gallon" originally meant "a large bowl," though this is one of the words whose parentage is quite unknown.

We speak now of an "exorbitant price," but the true meaning of the adjective is connected with "orbit" and therefore means "out of the track or circuit," while "extravagant," which to-day often means "wasteful," really means "wandering beyond."

"Vulgar" should mean simply "pertaining to the crowd," being from Latin *vulgus*, "the crowd," so that the Latin version of the Bible is called the Vulgate or the version published for the ordinary people. Cf. the expression "the vulgar tongue."

"To advertise" meant formerly merely "to make

known" and has only of late years been almost entirely connected with business announcements, and a " fable " in olden days was any story.

This process of specialisation is going on to-day in our midst, for we are inclined to speak of game as " birds " to the exclusion of other feathered creatures; we call turnips and carrots " roots," and many people call their maid-servant the " girl."

" The House " to some people always means " the Houses of Parliament," while to others it means " the Workhouse," just as the words " glass," " copper," " iron," have several different meanings, each used by some people in a specialised sense, for " copper " means one thing to the cook, another to the beggar, another to the metal worker, and another to those who give that name to the policeman, as a person who " cops "—that is, catches.

There are, again, some words which have, so to say, made a right-about turn and now mean just the opposite of what they did years ago. Take, for example, the word " restive " as applied to a horse and we now understand that the animal will not stand still, whereas it originally meant " quiet," " stubborn," coming, as it does, from the O.F. *restif*, from *rester*, " to remain."

You may have heard country people talk of " rusty bacon," meaning bacon that has " stood " too long; " rusty " is the same word as " restive,"

## SOME ANOMALIES IN ENGLISH

only it should be written "reasty," and we find the old meaning kept in the expression "to turn rusty" = "obstinate."

If we now say something is "quaint" we mean that it is unusual, but Shakespeare used it as meaning "pretty," "trim," and earlier still it meant "known," or "usual," being from the Latin *cognitus*, "known."

The German for "brave" is *tapfer* (Dutch *dapper*), and has given us our word "dapper," which carries with it little idea of courage; and no one would now care to be called "pert," though it originally meant "skilled in," from the Latin *expertus*, and has acquired its bad meaning from being confused with its opposite "malapert," now seldom used because supplanted by "pert."

"Bland" and "worthy" though really complimentary in meaning now convey an unpleasant impression, as does "smug," which is really the English form of the German *schmuck*, "elegant" or "beautiful."

Other words which have changed their meaning on being adopted into English are "knightly," which is the same as the German *knecht*, "servile," though *knecht* in High German of the Middle Ages meant "knight" as well as "servant." Grass is often called "greensward" in poetry, though the noun seldom stands alone without the adjective, and is really the same as the German *Schwarte,* the " sward " or rind of anything, especially of bacon.

" Pluck " used to be a slang word, while " arrant," now generally used only in a bad sense, as in " arrant knave," is really the French *errant,* " wandering," as in " knight-errant." " Unique " from Latin *unus, unicus,* "one," and meaning really " without equal," is losing its real meaning and is now often seen on goods in shop windows qualified by such terms as " very," " quite."

Of words which have lost a syllable, or perhaps more than one, there are a great number; some of these words were changed long ago, some are changing now, and the reason is generally laziness and a desire to avoid letters or combinations of letters which require some effort to pronounce, a good example of which is the disregard of *h* in French, for, even when it is written, it is not pronounced as it is in English.

In connection with this part of our subject it is interesting to note the preference shown by some nations for some sounds and their dislike of others. As a generalisation, we may say that the southern nations who inhabit warm climates prefer vowels, while those who dwell in the more inhospitable north use many hard consonants.

The Italians like soft sounds and so avoid certain consonants, putting *i* for *l,* and *r* and *z* for

# SOME ANOMALIES IN ENGLISH 127

*d* and *t*, as in *piano* for Latin *planus*, *mezzo* for Latin *medius*.

Together with *h*, the French dislike *l* and avoid a double consonant at the beginning of a word by putting *e* in front, thus making another syllable, as in O.F. *estincelle*, Mod. F. *étincelle* from the Latin *scintilla* (spark).

In the northern languages, however, we meet frequent groups of consonants that require some effort to pronounce and that the southern people find very difficult. We are so accustomed to them that we pronounce them without thinking; but look at the group of consonants in such words as "scratch," "strength," "thought," "Schloss" (Ger. castle), and you will see how much more effort is needed to pronounce them than is required for *casa* (It. house).

Though in many cases sounds have been changed by accident or popular mistake, or from carelessness and laziness, words that have travelled from one language to another have generally changed in obedience to rules called "sound laws." We will not here go into these rules, some of which are very complicated, but we will just notice, as we pass, the changes in the words we take as examples.

Sometimes it has been found that one sound is easier to pronounce when another is added, a fact to which we owe the *b* in such words as "slumber," "bramble," "nimble," which were formerly in

Anglo-Saxon *slūma, bremel, nimol*; and in the words coming from Latin as "humble" (*humilis*), "number" (*numerus*), "tomb" (*tumulus*). Instead of *b* we have *p* in "empty" (A.S. *æmtig*), and *d*, which seems to like to creep in when possible after *n*, in "thunder," (A.S. *thunor*), kindred (A.S. *kinred*), and you can hear any day among the less educated classes the result of this tendency when they say "gownd" (gown), "scholard" (scholar), "drownd" (drown).

*N* has somehow crept into the old forms *passager, messager*, and given us "passenger," "messenger"; while if you look at the Latin equivalents you will find that the *l* does not really belong to syllable, participle, principle.

The *r* does not belong to "hoarse" (A.S. *hās*), and "splash" should really be "plash."

Now the Anglo-Saxons had a great liking for guttural (throat) sounds, but the Normans had not, and, as the language of England changed gradually after the Norman Conquest, these gutturals dropped out by degrees; and perhaps it is as well, for they were very difficult to pronounce and not very pretty in sound. Thus, although we still write "thought" and "through," we do not pronounce the "gh" at all, neither do we in "caught," "high," or "plough."

This guttural *g* has disappeared from many words and been replaced by *i, y*, or *w*, as in "if" (A.S.

PLATE VIII—KNIFE WITH RUNIC ALPHABET OR "FUTHORC."

# SOME ANOMALIES IN ENGLISH

*gif*), "like" (A.S. *gelic*), "fair" (A.S. *faeger*), "rain" (A.S. *regen*), snail (A.S. *snagel*), "year" (A.S. *gear*), "body" (A.S. *bodig*), "sorrow" (A.S. *sorg*), and many others.

The Normans disliked *w*—in fact, they never used it, and, in any words they adopted from English or German, they changed an initial *w* into *g*. This accounts for the fact that the French for "William" is *Guillaume*, for "war" *guerre*, for "warden" *garde*, for "wafer" *gauffre*, though in some cases we have both words in English, as in "guile," "wile"; "guard," "ward"; "guise," "wise."

Sometimes letters have been dropped from the beginning of a word and thus a new word has been formed in addition to and with a different meaning from the first. Such are "defence," "fence"; "appeal," "peal"; "history," "story"; "distress," "stress"; "etiquette," "ticket"; "caravan," "van"; and the dropping process can be seen to-day in the forms "omnibus," "bus"; "although," "though"; "especial," "special."

Other words have been formed by the dropping of letters at the end instead of the beginning, as "canter," said to come from "Canterbury" (the pace of the Canterbury pilgrims); "cab" (cabriolet), "miss" (mistress); while others, again, are in the making, as "bike," "zoo," "cinema," "on spec," "on appro," "phone," and the forms "Bakerloo," "soccer," "rugger," and the 'Varsity "brunch" (breakfast and lunch as one meal).[1]

Just as these words have lost letters, so a few have gained letters, as in the case of "hermit" (Fr. *eremite*), "hazard" (Sp. *azar*), "newt" (from *an ewt*, "nickname" (*eke-name*).

In some cases letters have simply changed places, and you may be surprised to hear that when uneducated people say "waps" for "wasp," and "axed" for "asked," they are only using the forms used by our Anglo-Saxon forefathers, who said "grapsen" for "grasp," "claps" for "clasp," "thrid" for "third," and "brid" for "bird," a form found in Chaucer.

Many changes in words have come about through ignorance, and sometimes words are so much disguised that their first parents would hardly recognise them if they could see them to-day. Uneducated people hear a word, generally of foreign birth, which they do not know, but which has something of the sound of some other known word, and in the repetition of the form they make, a new word is born and adopted. This process can be easily seen in such words as the sixteenth- and seventeenth-century form "sparrow-

---

[1] The form "zoo" mentioned above is interesting as being not merely an abbreviation, but an abbreviation of a mispronunciation —the word "zoological" being apparently regarded as having only four syllables instead of five.

grass," which seems to have been almost normal and is still the gardener's name for asparagus; "brown-kitus" for "bronchitis"; and, forms which we ourselves have heard, such as "desecrated (desiccated) coco-nut," and "consecrated (concreted) pavement."

Examples of such words firmly established in the language are "Jerusalem artichoke," "Jerusalem" being the corruption of the French *girasole* = "turn to the sun"; "gilly-flower" from Fr. *giroflée*; "salt-cellar," Fr. *salière*; "Ember days" have nothing to do with ashes, but come from A.S. *ymber* = "a period"; and "humble pie" has nothing to do with humility, but carries our thoughts back to the days when lords and ladies, squires and servants dined all at one table in the banqueting hall. The gentles sat "above the salt"—that is, above the large salt-cellar which stood in the middle of the table—and they feasted on the choicest dishes, while the retainers sat "below the salt" and ate the umble pie, a pie made from the inferior portions of the venison. Of course the servants did occupy a humble position, so the *h* of the similar word was added to the noun "umble" and the whole expression "to eat humble pie" came to mean the unpleasant experience of being made to feel one's inferiority.

Among words which have travelled far and had romantic adventures we will mention a few of special interest.

Next time you go upstairs, just look at the banisters and remember that that word should really be "baluster" (just as we have "balustrade"), and that its original home was in Greece. The word in Greek means "a pomegranate" and apparently the knobs and other decorations usually seen on banisters were thought to resemble the wild pomegranate flower and so the name was born.

When we say a person is "bed-ridden" we are repeating an old English joke and calling some one who cannot leave his bed a "bed-rider" or "knight," where "ridden" is really a noun, whereas in "priest-ridden," an expression coined in imitation of the other, "ridden" is a participial adjective and the meaning is "under the thumb of the priesthood."

You would naturally connect "belfry" with the bell which hangs there, but it really has nothing to do with it except in the popular imagination. The word really means "watch-tower" and comes from two German words *berc* = "protection" (Mod. Ger. *bergen*) and *frid* (Mod. *Friede*) = "peace" = a tower or place of security.

If you did not know its history, you would never connect the word "trivial" with three Roman cross-roads, but that is its origin. Just as country people to-day meet to gossip in the market-place, whither all roads lead, so the Roman populace of old met for the same purpose at the cross-roads (Lat. *tria* =

"three"; *via* = "a way"), and hence the adjective *trivialis*, as applied to news or anything that is common or may be picked up anywhere, and therefore, in time, of little worth.

Except in company with brimstone, no one now thinks of treacle as connected with medicine, but the word comes from a Greek form meaning an antidote against the bites of serpents and in Middle English was always used to mean a sovereign remedy. Piers Plowman says that love is a " treacle (or cure) for sin," and Sir Thomas More calls miracles " a treacle against heresies "; and an ancient Greek or a medieval Englishman would be very surprised to find the name applied to the modern golden syrup and its darker relation.

The word " stocking " is a diminutive of *stock* and takes us back to the days when men wore doublet and hose, the latter a long garment that combined the purpose of trousers and stockings. Later, this garment was cut in two at the knees and divided into upper stocks and nether (lower) stocks, or stockings, " stocks " here meaning a piece or stump, a piece cut off.

Nowadays if a person shifts his position in an argument, or quibbles, we say he prevaricates, and this verb is used even of deliberate lying; but if traced to its origin in the remote past, we find it means " to be excessively bow-legged," and so " to walk crookedly," and was applied, in a Roman court of law, to an advocate who, while apparently prosecuting a man, was secretly in league with the other side to get him acquitted.

The words "mint" and "money" both come from Rome and belong to the goddess Juno, whom the Romans called *Juno Moneta*, "Juno the Adviser or Warner," and it was in her temple that money was coined. Juno reminds us of her husband Jupiter or Jove, and of the fact that, though few people now believe in the influence of the stars over human affairs, yet a man who is hopeful and cheerful by temperament is said to be "jovial" as having been born under the influence of the planet sacred to Jupiter. Just so, a man who is naturally gloomy is called "saturnine," or influenced by Saturn, the unlucky planet connected with the god of gloomy severity.

This belief in the influence of the stars is seen further in the words "mercurial" from the god Mercury, the quick-change artist of the gods; "disaster," a misfortune resulting from the influence of an unlucky star; "ill-starred," and "influence," which last word meant originally the influence of the planets.

A "lord" was, in Anglo-Saxon times, *hlafweard* = "the loaf-keeper," just as a "lady" was "the loaf-kneader," and the title "lady" in the term "our Lady" was specially used to mean the Virgin Mary, from whom are named the ladybird and lady's-slipper.

A heathen was not originally a person who worshipped false gods, but simply a dweller on the heath or open country. As, like all novelties, Christianity was first preached and practised in the towns, the country people received it much later in the days when travelling was difficult, so the term " heathman " or " heathen " came to mean " a person who was behind the times," and hence " one who did not follow the new religion." We find exactly the same history attached to the word " pagan," which is from Lat. *paganus*, " a dweller in the country," hence a follower of old and worn-out beliefs.

A " gooseberry " has nothing to do with geese, but means simply " a fruit with rough or curling hairs on it," from a Middle High German word *krus*, which appears in the French form *groseille*. Nowadays a costermonger may sell many things, but he is the modern representative of the " costard-monger " who sold " costards " or " apples," probably ribbed ones, from O.Fr. *costa*, Mod. Fr. *côte* = " rib."

You have probably never connected the high title of " Chancellor " with " crab," yet the first officers holding this position were so called because they sat behind a lattice-work like crossed crab's-claws, the Latin for " crab " being *cancer*, dim. *cancellus*. " To cancel " means " to cross out by drawing lines across like lattice-work." An "attic" is now a small upper room, but the term was originally applied to the whole of a parapet wall which ended the upper face of a building and is named from the Attic style of architecture.

"Court cards" were in former times called "coat cards" because the king, queen, and knave wore long robes; a "cynic" is really a dog-like person, or a snarler, while the term "supercilious" comes from two Latin words, *super* = above, and *cilium* = eyebrow, and means "haughty" because disdain is frequently shown by raising the eyebrows.

So we might add to the list almost indefinitely, and the more words we examined, the more we should wonder at the history contained in language, and there are few more fascinating occupations than turning over the leaves of some good etymological dictionary and tracing out the life-story of the words we use each day.

## CHAPTER VI

#### METAPHOR IN EVERYDAY SPEECH

HAVE you ever realised how many of the expressions we use in our daily life are metaphors or little word-pictures drawn from many sources, carrying us back in thought to days of old and to far-away lands, but which we have used and heard so often that we have forgotten the original and thus lose much of the charm and picturesqueness that lie hidden in our everyday speech?

If you once begin to note these little word-pictures you will be astonished at the frequency with which you use them unthinkingly. In fact, you can hardly speak half-a-dozen sentences without one coming to "the tip of your tongue"; which last expression is itself a picture.

Suppose we look at some of these everyday metaphors; space will not allow of our mentioning more than a few, but you will be able to add to the list if you care to do so.

Some of these metaphors consist of one word, or perhaps two, while others are longer expressions and have become almost proverbs. A *key*, for instance, means first an instrument that unlocks, and from that we go on to apply the term to the solution of a problem and a book containing many such solutions. As a *branch* is an offshoot of a tree, we have formed metaphors by talking of the branch of a family, of a business, a branch of learning, of a special subject, or of an institution.

So, too, with the idea of running water in our mind, we say that our thoughts flow; we reap the reward of our actions; we are goaded by ambition; our eyes flame and hopes are kindled, quenched, or shattered. We can speak of an upright man, a striking thought, a threadbare argument, and of being fettered by poverty; while we can say that a person's mind wandered, his reason tottered, or his faith failed.

Most of these metaphors are formed of nouns, verbs, or adjectives, but we can make them also of prepositions and adverbs, as in the expressions, what are you after? beneath contempt; under chloroform; to speak fluently.

We can talk of grasping an idea, of handling a subject, and of letting fall a hint; of a sweet voice, a rough tone, rugged features; and, nine times out of ten, we do not think of the first and original meaning of the expressions.

These little metaphors are always full of vigour and much more expressive than any more literal paraphrase. Think of the vividness of such terms as

# METAPHOR IN EVERYDAY SPEECH 139

piercing screams, crying evils, a lightning glance, frowning mountains, knitted brows, burying resentment, raking up old troubles.

When we say that a person is fretting we are unconsciously recalling the biblical expression of "a moth fretting a garment," where "fret" means "to eat up," from the A.S. *fretan*, "to eat away," used of animals in distinction from the word *etan*, "to eat," used of human beings, this distinction being still retained in the German *essen*, "to eat" (of people), *fressen*, "to eat" (of animals).

In like manner we can speak of a gnawing pain or anxiety; and of carking care, where "carking" is from a Mid. E. word *karke*, "a load," as in the expression "a karke of pepper."

What ideas do the words "flap" and "crack" convey to you? Do they call up any picture to the mind's eye?—the expression "the mind's eye" being itself a metaphor, you will note. The word "flap" should carry your thoughts (another metaphor!) to the days of long, long ago when one of our early ancestors sat on the shore, or in his primitive boat, and heard the sound of a blow on some flat surface, either the movement of a bird's wing or the corner of a sail. If you repeat the word "flap" to yourself, you can see it all. The word was then applied to the movement to and fro of a flat surface and then to any part of a flat surface that was movable, as the leaf of a table, and all visible connection with the sound was lost.

The word " crack " imitates the sound of a hard body breaking and is applied in a secondary sense to the effects of that breaking, then to the separation of broken parts or to a narrow separation between broken edges, so that now, when we speak of the crack of the door or a crack in the wall, the idea of sound never enters our mind. As an interesting example of the secondary meanings of words, let us look at the word " point " and you will, I think, be astonished to find that there are at least twenty-five separate meanings as given below, and more might be added. One day when you have nothing to do you might amuse yourself by writing down the extended meanings of such words as *head, line, way, power*.

1. The first meaning of " point " is a sharp end, as of a pin or needle.
2. From that we apply the term to any object that tapers, as a sword.
3. A point is an etching tool, as when we say " drawn with the point."
4. In printing, a point is a projecting pin on a press for marking the register.
5. On the railway a point is a movable switch at junctions.

## METAPHOR IN EVERYDAY SPEECH

6. The punch used by stone masons is called a point.
7. A branch of a deer's antlers is a point.
8. In backgammon a point is one of the narrow, tapering spaces on which the men are placed.
9. Points, to a bookbinder, are stout needles on a flat board on which the printed sheets are placed so that the edges may be cut exactly.
10. In geography a point is a cape.
11. The most noticeable feature or physical peculiarity—points of a dog.
12. The chief feature of a story.
13. The precise question in dispute—"let us come to the point."
14. A detail, "at all points."
15. Purpose, end, or aim—"to gain one's point."
16. A mark or dot to denote separation.
17. Decimal point.
18. An object having position but not magnitude.
19. Precise degree or limit—"boiling point."
20. Small unit of measurement.
21. Unit of fluctuation in price of shares—"gone up 200 points."
22. Unit of count in a game.
23. In piquet a point is the number of cards in the longest suit of a hand.
24. A term in lace-making—"needle-point."
25. A cricket fielder.

These are the chief meanings of the word "point," but even this long list might be extended.

Now let us look at some metaphors that fall into classes, as they are connected with some particular subject as the sea, sport, old customs, the classics, etc.

As we were originally a nation of sea-rovers and still remain so to a large extent, we are not surprised to find that we daily use a number of little word-pictures connected with the sea.

We say, for instance, that an angry person storms or rages and then calms down; we talk of the ship of State, and call a statesman the pilot, and, if times are troubled, we say there are breakers ahead and hope that he will steer us through and weather the storm successfully.

You have often heard life compared with a voyage, and man's life is spoken of as a frail bark, while death is pictured as a crossing of the bar or the entering into a desired haven.

When you are bewildered and wonder which way to turn, you say you are all at sea; and if a man has difficulty in making both ends meet, you say he can scarcely keep his head above water, and, if he fails, he goes under. Happiness can be wrecked and care drowned, and when things are lost they go by the board.

A woman is said to sail into a room as a yacht

in smooth waters, and the waves of light or sound undulate, or move, as waves of the sea; hair is wavy, and a person who speaks by the card should really carry our thoughts to the ship's compass or chart.

Boys at play, or thieves and other evil-doers, make use of the expression " the coast is clear," as did the smugglers of days gone by, but not all those who nail their colours to the mast, or haul them down, are sailors.

It is quite possible to tack and to launch out without ever having been in a boat, just as you can paddle your own canoe though you know nothing about the art in its primary sense.

When you take a holiday you rest on your oars, though you may be preparing " to take arms against a sea of troubles," in which expression Shakespeare has used a mixed metaphor—one picture being taken from the battlefield and the other from the sea.

Though we certainly never think of it when we use the words, " opportune" and "inopportune" were originally connected with the timely arrival or non-arrival of ships at a port.

So much for ships, sailors, and the sea!

You will remember that it was to the splendid archery of the stout yeomen of England that Edward III owed his victories in France, and, as late as Tudor days, all the men of a village were accustomed to practise with bow and arrow on the village green each Sunday after the church service.

Archery has long since become a thing of the past with us, but we still use many expressions which carry our minds back to the feats of Robin Hood and his merry men, and still farther back to the time when Cupid first worked his will in the sunny lands of Greece. Though we shoot no more with the bow, we say that a thing goes as straight as an arrow; we hit the mark, the target, or the bull's-eye without ever having handled a bow. When someone tells a marvellous tale, we accuse him of drawing the long bow, for no doubt an archer made the most of his achievements then as do sportsmen and fishermen of theirs to-day; and if anyone earns some distinction, we say that he has a feather in his cap, such as Robin Hood won at the Sheriff's contest at Nottingham.

The father of a large family is said to have his quiver full, and a woman who encourages more than one admirer has two strings to her bow.

"Aim" has not necessarily any connection with a target as it once had, nor have the expressions "beside the mark," "to overstep the mark," "point-blank," "blank" being the modern form of "blanc" (white) = the bull's-eye.

So, though we had no written record of the good old days, these expressions should still keep alive in our minds pictures of life and customs in the Merrie England of long ago.

Of metaphors drawn from war there are quite a number in our language, as you will realise with very little reflection. We speak of the sinews of war (a double metaphor), the honours of war, and of flying colours, with no thought of war in our mind.

It is not necessary to be a soldier to be up in arms, to take up arms, or to mark time; and you can stand to your guns even though you know nothing of artillery. When we talk of sticking to one's colours, taking by storm, losing or gaining ground, we are talking in military language, just as we are when we say " that is half the battle." The expression "to be under the heel" of anyone is one that has survived from the days when the conqueror placed his foot upon the fallen foe in token of victory; and when we say some one is "worth his salt" we are unconsciously borrowing from the Roman soldier, part of whose daily pay was a portion of salt, a custom which gives us our word " salary" or " salt money."

If anything passes muster now we do not at once assume that it has been before the military authorities, nor is everyone who hangs out the red flag a republican insurgent.

Though the days of chivalry have long since passed, we still recall the custom of throwing down the glove or gauntlet by way of challenge and of picking it up in acceptance of that challenge, when we speak of throwing down the gauntlet or taking up the challenge. In modern days we run the gauntlet of public opinion or criticism, which, though perhaps unpleasant enough, is not physically painful as was the ordeal which gave birth to the expression; for in olden times a prisoner, stripped to the waist, had to run between two lines of soldiers armed with gloves (sometimes of steel), sticks, and other weapons, with which they struck him as he passed. This word " gauntlet " though confused with the one above is really different, being a corruption of " gantlope " (*gata* = " lane," *lopp* = " course "). We still speak of a trying ordeal, but seldom, if ever, connect the expression with ordeal of fire or water which accused persons had to undergo before the days of judge and jury.

Have you ever realised how many metaphors are connected with animals? We call a greedy person a pig; a stupid person a donkey; an obstinate person a mule; a cross-grained person (metaphor from wood) a bear. Few people would care to be called a cat, fond as they may be of an animal which is really very dignified and graceful; while " duck " is a term of endearment though the bird has an ungainly walk and an unmusical voice. In Germany *beetle, worm,* and even *flea* are terms of endearment;

# METAPHOR IN EVERYDAY SPEECH 147

Prospero called Miranda " poor worm," and the French say " my little cabbage."

The expression " a gay bird " is easily accounted for, but why " a gay dog " ? The uncomplimentary meaning of " you dog ! " and " go to the dogs " must surely have come from the East, where the lean scavenger dogs prowl about the streets uncared for and reviled, unlike their English brothers. Note also in this connection the degrees of contempt in the terms " hound " and " cur " applied to people.

A near-sighted person is a bat or an owl; a very gentle person a lamb; a crafty person a fox, while one has unfortunately met women whose waspish tempers have earned them, strangely enough, the name of vixen.

If you are busy and energetic you are a bee; if lazy and indolent, a drone; if thirsty, a fish; and when you call anyone cold-blooded you are thinking of animals such as the snake, tortoise, and lizard.

That a person should object to being called a reptile is easily understood; and though Shakespeare speaks in *As You Like It* of the precious jewel thought of old to be worn in the head of the toad, he also shows us in *Macbeth* how the connection of that animal with witches gave rise to the contempt of the expressions " you toad," and " to toady."

Everyone has, when a child, capered with delight, that is, danced as a goat, but few people would, at any age, care to be called a goat; elephant, jackass, and ape are scarcely complimentary epithets; but monkey is almost a term of endearment, especially when qualified by " little "; giraffe is harmless and lion is entirely complimentary.

The term " gull " is hard on the bird, for the expression is probably quite unconnected with it, coming most likely from a verb meaning " to swallow greedily "; but the vanity and self-satisfaction of the cock is perhaps sufficient to prevent him from caring much for the reflections cast on his character by the expressions " cocky " and " cock of the walk."

Men, as well as bulls, bellow; people have been known to bill and coo as doves, and you have heard a buzz of conversation and a roar of applause. A leisurely person is a snail, and we can draw in our horns though we have no shell on our back; people, as well as horses, are put through their paces, and most people at some time in their life have felt like a fish out of water. Men are said to feather their nest, and our hopes sometimes soar high, while high-flyers were known before aeroplanes were invented.

Some of the metaphors connected with animals have also to do with sport so-called. From fox-hunting we get the expressions " to be in at the death," " to run to earth," " hue and cry after," " full cry after," while " in the long run " may conceivably have had more than one origin.

"To set by the ears" has to do with dog-fights, perhaps also from bear-baiting, which gives us "to bait"; we say some one is badgered, though it was the poor badger that was badgered, and we dog a person's footsteps or hound a villain out of the country.

"To reclaim" originally meant to call back a hawk in the days of royal hawking-parties, and though now it is horses which are kept in a mews the nobles of old kept their falcons there when moulting; the French for "to moult" being *muer*, from which we have made "mews."

Most people have been on a wild-goose chase at some time or other, but no one would care to be accused of running with the hare and hunting with the hounds.

When we say that Belgium is the cock-pit of Europe we unconsciously recall the favourite pastime of our fathers, cock-fighting, which has given us also the expressions "crestfallen," "to live like fighting cocks," and "to show the white feather," which last refers to the belief that no bird that was a good fighter had ever been known to possess a white feather in its plumage.

Metaphors which have grown up round colours are very interesting and their origin is not always very easy to trace.

"To see red" and "to be caught red-handed"

are of course easily connected with the colour of blood, and one can easily understand the feeling that gave rise to such terms as " black humour," " black looks," " black books," " black sheep."

A green person is one who is immature and therefore easily taken in, though why jealousy should be called the green-eyed monster is not easily seen, nor why that feeling should be indicated by yellow, unless it was from the idea prevailing in the Middle Ages that love resided not in the heart but in the liver, whence our expression " a jaundiced view of things."

Everyone is cheered by the sight of a blue sky, but a depressed person has the blues, and when fortune favours, it is a blue look-out. We all like to be seen through rose-coloured glasses, and a rosy view of things is sometimes pleasant; but why should a person sunk in thought (another metaphor) be said to be in a brown study ?

There are a number of metaphors which have passed into our language from the Bible, which being really an Eastern book is full of word-pictures, yet how often we use these expressions with no thought of their origin ! When we say that we wash our hands of somebody do we ever think of Pilate who washed his hands before the people as a token that he took no responsibility in the condemnation of Christ ? Few good Samaritans have been anywhere

## METAPHOR IN EVERYDAY SPEECH 151

near Samaria, just as a man can put his hand to the plough without ever having been on a farm. We call children " olive branches," and speak of the eleventh hour, of girding up our loins, of casting pearls before swine, of pouring oil on troubled waters ; we name an old cabman a Jehu in derision ; a friend who depresses rather than comforts is a Job's comforter, while the scapegoat and the wolf in sheep's clothing are known to most of us.

Fables have given us " sour grapes," " a dog in the manger," " borrowed plumes," and to the Classics we owe many expressions whose original meaning is quite unknown to many who use them.

Some such are " the sword of Damocles," which hung by a single hair over the head of a flatterer to prove how frail is the security of kings ; and " a Parthian shot," which now consists of words, was originally the arrow skilfully shot by the Parthians as they retreated swiftly on their horses. We still cut Gordian knots, but it was Alexander the Great who cut the first one, and, following the example of Caesar, we cross the Rubicon when we take a decisive step, or, as an alternative, we burn our boats. The torture of Tantalus is still brought before our minds in the verb " to tantalise," and the endless stone-rolling of the king of Corinth in the expression "a Sisyphean task," while " Herculean task," " Argus-eyed " are often used.

To music we owe such metaphors as "highly-strung," "unstrung," as applied to nerves; and "in tune," "out of tune," "discord," "accord," "prelude," "harmony," all belong strictly speaking to music but are now used with other meanings. A person can be as fit as a fiddle and yet have no knowledge of violin-playing, just as he can play second fiddle and know nothing of music.

The number of unclassified metaphors is legion, and each one has grown and been adopted into the language because of its inherent picturesqueness and force of expression.

There is no need to be a carpenter to insert the thin end of the wedge, nor a blacksmith to have several irons in the fire or strike while the iron is hot; nor is it really necessary to know the three R's to enable one to read between the lines.

A person who was leading another a pretty dance, though unable really to dance a step, might be laughing up his sleeve all the time, and some people cannot put two and two together though good at arithmetic, nor can they see events that take place under their very nose.

Everyone can stand in his own light, though it is impossible to be in two places at once, and yet, on the other hand, you can be beside yourself with rage.

It would be quite possible, too, to put your best

leg foremost even though you had not a leg to stand on, and to open the eyes of some one whose eyes were apparently wide open at the time; just as you can turn up your nose at something, though that feature is a beautiful Grecian type. Most people have broken the ice in the summer and taken the bull by the horns in a drawing-room, and a carter who harnesses his steed every day may frequently put the cart before the horse.

A person who is out at elbows can seldom make ends meet, and, even if he has not a leg to stand on, would be glad to be set on his feet. People who play with edged tools generally come to grief though they may not actually cut themselves, and others have been known to make ducks and drakes with their money though that generally happens in town and not at the water's edge.

In the literal sense it would be difficult to burn the candle at both ends, and in the metaphorical sense it does not pay, while many really kind-hearted people could be accused of throwing dust in the eyes of others.

We might go on quoting familiar metaphors at any length, but we have mentioned enough to show how large a part of our everyday speech they form. Paraphrase any set of metaphors and you will see atonce how much force of expression and picturesqueness is lost; in fact, so well do familiar metaphors express what is in one's mind, that you will find it very difficult to put that thought into other words.

It would not, perhaps, be too much to say that almost every word we use is a metaphor, and if you, like Theseus in the maze, have followed the thread of this chapter, we hope that you will be ready to admit that our everyday speech is fuller of colour, interest and romance than you ever thought before.

# CHAPTER VII

### PLACE NAMES

HAVE you ever realised that every geographical name was once a word, just a descriptive word, and has a history of its own thrilling with the romance of age and many adventures ? Of all words perhaps those which have come down to us as geographical names, especially local names, are the oldest and have undergone the least change on their journey. Words have indeed proved stronger and more enduring than the great works of man—the cities and temples he built have often long since perished, but their name and story, enshrined in *words*, live on when the nation which first spoke those words has ceased to exist.

These words, often lost to the more educated, survive in the language of the peasant who thus unconsciously uses the very names and phrases of his early forefathers. Without the light thrown on the past by the study of local names, history, geology, and other kindred subjects would impart less than they do of the early history of man and the world; and by a careful search into the local names of a country, it is possible to tell a great deal of its history.

Many of these long-lived names are, or were at first, merely descriptive, as in the case of *Snowdon*, *Ben Nevis* (Snow Mountain), *Mont Blanc* (White Mountain), and, in the case of places where nature has changed in appearance, owing to the clearing of forests, the draining of marshes, the filling up of lakes, or the alterations of coast-line, these old descriptive names are of great value.

Sometimes geographical names support the evidence of history, as in the case of *Londonderry*, so called because resettled by the London guilds; *Queen's County* and *King's County*, with their county towns of *Maryborough* and *Philipstown*, remind us that they were colonised by the English in the reign of Mary I; *Adelaide* in South Australia was called after the wife of William IV; *Rhodesia* after Cecil Rhodes, while anyone could think of a dozen more such examples off-hand, though some are now much disguised, and you might not think that *Wansdyke*, for instance, was once *Woden's Dyke*.

Let us now look at some well-known geographical names and see what stories they have to tell us of people and days of long ago, keeping largely to our own islands as being best known to us.

Now though the Celts (of whom we spoke in our first chapter) did not write their history, they have left us many records behind them in the names they gave to places, not [only in England, but in

Scotland, Ireland, the Isle of Man, Wales, and France.

Of all the various classes of local names you will find that the names of rivers, especially of important ones, are the oldest—we might almost say that they never die. The towns on their banks may long ago have been destroyed, the country round may have been deserted and ravaged and all other traces of the early inhabitants wiped out, yet the name of the river given to it by the first settlers will live on.

We speak sometimes of the " eternal hills," but even their names are less enduring than those of the ever-flowing rivers.

If we examine the river names of Europe we find that in almost all cases the names are Celtic, and in England there is hardly a stream whose name is not of that origin. These Celtic river-names are chiefly of two classes—the first *substantival*, the second *adjectival* or descriptive.

The names belonging to the first class are very old words that simply mean *river* or *water*, being as we have mentioned before, at first ordinary words. In the early days when the land was covered with dense forests and there were no real roads, people did not travel about except for short distances on foot, hunting, or in tiny boats fishing. Geographical knowledge therefore would be very slight, and whole tribes would know only one river, which to them would be *The River*, or *The Water*, so that at first these names were just ordinary words and only became proper names when some foreign race conquered the tribe and misunderstood the general term *The Water* to be the special name for that particular stream.

Take, for example, the word *afon*, which is the Welsh for "river." At Bettws-y-Coed is the *Afon Llugwy*, which is in English "the river Llugwy," and on the map of Wales you will find many other examples of this word *afon*. Now the incoming Northmen drove the Celts out of England to a large extent, but the conquered race left memorials behind them, one of them being their word *afon*. The Northmen or English, however, took this to be a proper name for a certain river, pronounced it as *avon*, and now all over England we find a large number of rivers of varying sizes called *Avon* as a proper name, notably, of course, the river that Shakespeare knew so well, and the *Avons* of Bristol and Hampshire.

We can go farther than this and say that in all the countries of Europe where the Celts once lived we find this name of *afon*, its appearance slightly changed owing to the passage of centuries and ill-treatment from strange tongues, but it is possible still to see its resemblance to its first parent.

We find it as *Avon* or *Evan* in Scotland, as *Ive* in Cumberland, *Inn* in Scotland and Tyrol; as

*Aune* in Devon, and in Ireland as the *Aven-more*. In France we find it as an ending now slightly changed to *on*, as in *Madon*, *enne* as in *Mayenne*, *onne*, *Garonne*, *one* in *Saone*, while in *Drave* and *Save*, tributaries of the Danube, we have the first part of the Celtic word preserved. Lastly, we have in Portugal the *Avia*, and in Italy the *Avens*, though these are only a very few of the Avon family.

Another Celtic word appearing in many river names is the Welsh *dwr* = "water," descended from which we have the proper names *Dour, Duir, Adur, Cheddar, Lodore, Dee, Dove, Derby*.

The Gaelic and Erse word for water is *uisge* (which gives us whisky) and it appears in the names *Esk Exe, Axe, Ux*, the last being a good example of the survival of the Celtic river name, though it was transferred to the town on its banks, *Uxbridge*, where the Romans renamed the river *the Colne*. In Spain we have the *Esca*, in France the *Aès* or *Aèse*, and *Aisne* (originally *Axona*), and in Germany *Etch*bach, *Asch*bach, and others.

It happens sometimes that a river name is found composed of two parts, each of which means *river* or *stream*, for when the conquering race asked the name of a stream and were told it was *dwr* or *afon*, they took that to be a proper name and added to it their own name for stream, as in the case of the *Durbeck* in Notts, *dwr* being, as we have seen, the

Celtic for "water," and *beck* (Mod. Ger. *bach*) from the Icelandic *bekkr* "stream," so that the modern name really means, "water-water" or "river-river."

Let us now look at a few Celtic river names belonging to the second or descriptive class.

The Welsh word *garw* means "rough," and, remembering that the old English *g* was often pronounced like *y*, we shall see the origin of such names as *Yare*, *Yarrow*, *Garonne*, *Garrow*, while the Gaelic *all* = "white" gives us *Allen*, *Allan*, *Alan*, *Ellen*, *Ilen*, *Aln*, and *Aulne*. From *ban* also meaning "white" we have *Bann*, *Bandon*, *Banny*, and *Bannockburn*, and from *llwn*, "smooth," or *linn*, "a deep smooth pool," we get *Loch Leven*, the rivers *Line*, *Leaven*, and the towns (by the pool) of *King's Lynn*, *Dublin*, *Linlithgow*, and probably *London*, the fort by the marsh or pool.

*Tam*, "wide and spreading," gives us *Thames*, *Tamas*, *Taff*, *Tone*, and from *cam* = "crooked" we have of course *Cam*, this word still being used in the Manchester dialect, and it is found in Shakespeare's *Coriolanus* where Menenius says "This is clean cam" = quite crooked.

We know very little of the origin of our mountain names—*Pennine*, for instance is quite a mystery—but many of them mean simply "height," the most usual Celtic word being *pen*, "a head," as *Pennigant*, *Penhill*, the latter being named "hill" twice over.

PLATE IX.—OGAM INSCRIPTION.

In the north of Scotland we find the same word spelt *ben*, as *Ben More*, but in the south we have *Pentland*, *Penpont*, *Pencraig*, and, by noticing where the Cymric or Welsh form *pen* changes into the Gaelic or Highland form *ben*, we can tell where these different branches of the Celtic race settled.

*Tor*, meaning " a tower-like hill," is another frequent name for heights, especially in the south-west of England, as *Hey Tor*, *Hare Tor* in Devon, while *craig*, " a rock," very common in Wales, appears in *Cricklade* and as *Carrick* with compounds in Ireland.

There are very few inlets with Celtic names except *Humber*, an aspirated form of *Cumber* from Welsh *cymmex*, " a confluence," and the *Solent*, which perhaps contains the Celtic *sol*, " tide."

Many names of towns and villages are Celtic in origin: *London* we have mentioned; *York* is from *Eborach*, a Saxon respelling of Celtic *Eburach* = place of the marsh; the Danes turned this into *Jorvik*, which, as the *j* was pronounced as *y*, soon became *York*. *Carlisle* was " the castle of Liol," *Truro* was " three ways" because built at the junction of three main roads.

*Dover* is on the R. Douver (fr. W. *drofe* = " stream"), so that the French pronunciation *Douvres* is correct, and we find a place of that name in the north of France.

Celtic names occur in any numbers in ten counties

only, Northumberland, Cumberland, Lancashire, Cheshire, Shropshire, Hereford, Monmouth, Somerset, Dorset, and Cornwall, whereas in Norfolk and Suffolk, Cambridge, Huntingdon, and Hertford there are practically none.

The names of a few counties contain a Celtic root to which a Latin suffix has been added, as in *Leicester*, the camp on the river Leir, the old name for the Soar. *Gloucester* and *Lancashire* probably also belong to this class.

We have, of course, mentioned only a few of the names that have come down to us from the Celts, but enough to show how enduring such names have proved, and a study of the names of continental countries where the Celts once lived would only serve to strengthen that proof.

Let us look now a little at the few names that the Romans left us as the result of their stay in England of 365 years. Seeing that they lived here so long it may be rather surprising that they left so little trace on the map, but we must remember that there were comparatively few Romans compared with the native Britons; all the natural features had long since been named, and the Roman civilisation was, in this case, superficial and transitory, and being military, not domestic, all disappeared before the incoming hordes of English.

The chief legacy of the Romans is to be found in

the ending *caster, chester, cester*, from the Latin *castra,* "a camp," a suffix which suffered rather interesting changes when the Northmen came. Thus in the districts where the Saxons alone settled, as Essex, Sussex, Wessex, we find it spelt as *Chester* as in *Colchester, Rochester, Winchester*, but as we pass to Anglian and Danish territory—Norfolk, Suffolk, and the Midlands—we find the form *caster*, as in *Doncaster, Tadcaster*, and this change can be seen very clearly by following the course of the river Nen, which divides the Danish Northamptonshire from the Saxon Huntingdon. On the Saxon side of the river is a village called *Chesterton,* and on the Danish bank is a town *Castor*, telling us of the old ford guarded by two Roman camps. In the old kingdom of Mercia (the Midlands), where Saxons and Angles mingled, we find the form *cester* with a great tendency to omit the *e*, for we have *Bicester* (pronounced Bister), *Worcester* (Wuster), *Gloucester* (Gloster).

Up in the north, where the Danes did not penetrate but the Saxons did, we have the long Saxon form *Chester, Lanchester, Ribchester*, and towards the Welsh border the *ch* becomes *x* as *Exeter* (originally Excester), *Wroxeter, Uttoxeter* (Uxter or Uxeter).

In almost all these names with a Latin suffix the first syllable is Celtic, as in *Exeter, Dorchester* (fr. C. *uisge* and *dwr* = "water") and thus are linked together in our minds the memories of two nations—of which the language of the conquered in this case has proved more enduring than that of the conquerors.

Other place names that recall the Romans are the term *le Street*, as in *Chester-le-Street, Stratton, Streatly*, reminding us of the wonderful Roman roads that still remain all over England and the names *Wallsend, Heddon-on-the-Wall, Walltown, Wallhead*, occurring along the line of the wall built by Hadrian from Newcastle to Carlisle.

After the Romans left England, these islands were ravaged by the Northmen—Jutes, Angles, Saxons, and Danes, all of whom have left traces on the map of to-day. The original Anglian speech is now best represented by that of the Lowland Scot and the burr of the northern miner; and before 1400 the same tongue was spoken from Hull to Aberdeen. We will notice now a few of the more distinctive Anglian or Early English legacies in our place names.

You will find that most of our town and village names are English, for it is typical of the race, even in those early times, that the Englishman thought much of his home, so that *ham*, " home," and *ton* " town," are frequent endings. Sometimes the *ham* represents the A.S. *ham*, " house " or " home " (cf. Ger. *heim*) and has generally as prefix a personal name as *Lewisham, Rockingham*, and at others it is from A.S. *ham* or *hom*, " an enclosure," as *Farnham, Twickenham, Evesham*.

*Ton*, " a town," originally " a homestead," is generally preceded by some descriptive word, as in *Newton*, of which there are 129 examples in England; *Sutton, Norton, Weston*, named from the points of the compass are also frequent, and *Easton*, which appears now as *Aston*. We have also *Middleton*, sometimes contracted to *Melton* and *Milton*, and names showing relative position as *Upton, Overton, Hampton* (the high town). Besides these suffixes we have *bury*, appearing as *borough* and *burgh*, and also *berry*, *bur*, and *bee*, though sometimes these may be from the A.S. *beorg, beorh*, " a hill." Thus *Knaresborough* in Yorkshire shows the form *burg*, " a town," but *Riseborough*, in the same county, has the suffix *beorg*, " hill."

Among other Anglo-Saxon suffixes we have *ley* or *lea*, a meadow, as in *Wembley, Stanley*, and in another form as in *Leigh, Bickleigh*; *hall* or *hale* (flat land by a river) gives us *Ticknall, Buxhall, Rushall*; and *mer* (a mere) appears in *Cromer, Walmer*.

As a rule the suffix *ing* is a patronymic, as in the case of the *Æscings*, the royal family of Kent, but it has also a geographical meaning, too, as in *Centings*, the *men* of Kent, *Bromleagings*, the men of Bromley. Names having the suffix *stone* show that at one time some memorial stone stood there as in *Bishopstone*, and *Kinwardstone*, while *Chipping*, found in compounds as *Chipping Norton, Chipping Barnet*, means "a place of sale" (A.S. *céap*, "cattle" or "market"), and *Staple*, as in *Stapleton, Barnstaple*, denoted a post or pillar of wood or stone put up in markets and other places where goods might be put out for sale.

Other Anglo-Saxon elements in place names are *barrow*, "a wood," or wooded hill, *cot* or *cote*, "a thatched cottage," usually appearing only in the names of very small places; *ridge, dic,* or *dike*, "a ditch"; *field*, meaning "any open land," and *den*, "a woodland."

Our other settlers, the Vikings, have also left many records behind them in our place names, and, by knowing the chief test words which appear in these names, we can follow the track of their raids in these islands.

As is to be expected, by far the larger number of these names occur within the Danelagh and of the counties in that district. Lincoln is the most Scandinavian, Yorkshire and Rutland follow very closely behind, while Huntingdon, Bedford, Cambridge, and Hertford have comparatively few.

The most useful test words are *thorpe*, as in *Bishopsthorpe, Althorpe*, the suffix meaning "village" and occurring 63 times in Yorkshire. *By* or *byr* meant "a dwelling-place," hence a "town or village," which meaning gives us the word *by-law*.

*Thwaite* is distinctly Norse and means "a clearing

in a forest"; it is to be found frequently in Cumberland and not once in Lincoln, whereas *thorpe*, which is Danish, occurs at least 63 times in Lincoln and only once in Cumberland.

Other northern suffixes are *force* or *foss* ("a waterfall"), *haugh, dale,* and *fell.*

But the Vikings did not all settle down in England and forsake their roving ways; many of them sailed round the coast of our islands, leaving traces of their visits which we can see to-day.

The suffix *ford* is found inland all over the country, indicating the place at which our Anglo-Saxon forefathers forded the river at its shallowest point; but the suffix *ford* occurs, too, in names round the coast, as *Milford, Wexford,* and in these cases the suffix represents the Norse *fiord,* a narrow passage up into the land where ships could sail for trade or plunder.

Other traces of the Northmen are to be found in such terms as *ness, scar, holm,* and *ey* (*oe, a, ay*), examples of which are to be found all round our coasts, as in the *Naze, Fife Ness, Scarborough, Jersey.*

With these test words in our minds let us follow the path of the Northmen round our shores and notice a few places that they touched at so long ago.

Starting from the capital, we know from the *Anglo-Saxon Chronicle* that the Danes attacked London several times and, it may be, left records behind in the names *Deptford* (deep ford), *Greenwich,* and *Woolwich*. The spits and headlands all along the east coast from London to Sutherland are frequently northern in name, as in the case of *Sheerness*, the *Naze*, *Harwich*, near which place there must have been a colony of Danes, for we find such names as *Harwich*, *Thorpe-le-Soken*, *East Thorpe*, *Kirby*, and others.

In Suffolk we find *Ipswich*, *Walberswick*, *Thorpe*, while Norfolk teems with Scandinavian names, two of the most interesting being *Repps* (near Cromer), recalling the Norse word *hrepp*, a rope, which was used to name a division of land marked out by these means, and *S. Olave's Bridge*, which reminds us of the royal saint of the Norse peoples, whose name, sadly mutilated, appears also in *Tooley Street*.

As we go north the names become more distinctively Danish, especially in Yorkshire, but north of that again they are fewer and found on the coast, which fact tells us that the Vikings touched here and there for trade or plunder, but did not settle.

But sail up to the north-east corner of Scotland and a surprise awaits you, for you will find that the names in that part of the mainland and in the Orkneys and Shetlands are very largely Norwegian.

Why is it that the most northerly county in the United Kingdom is called *Sutherland*, the South Land ? Have you ever wondered at that in looking at the map of Scotland ? Surely the Scots would not

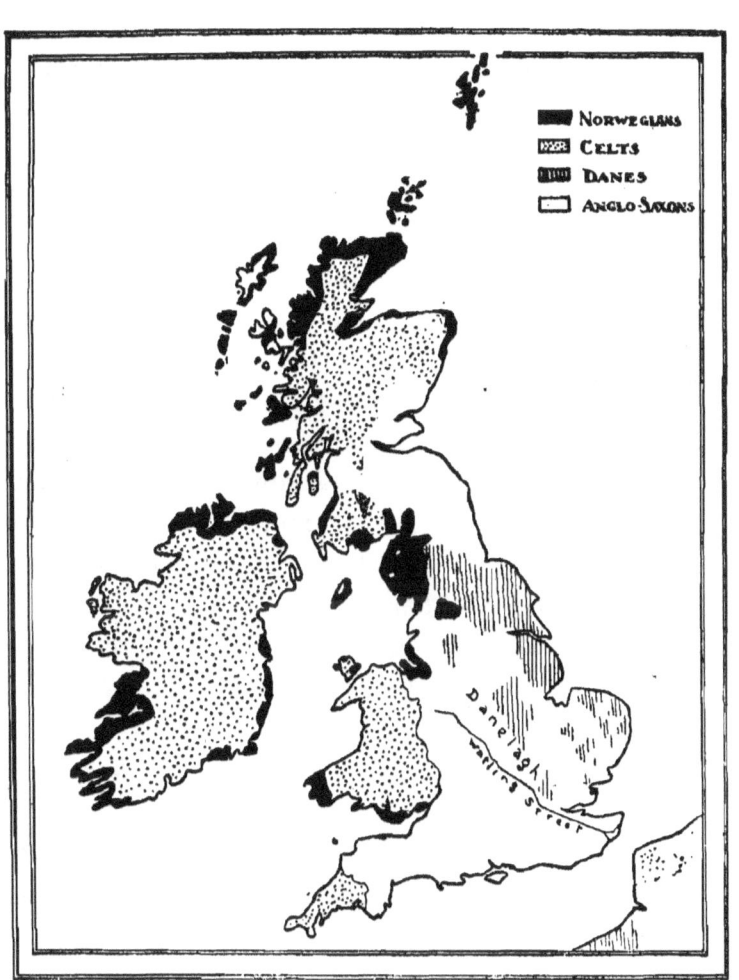

have called it that? No, the fact is that the local names of the district bear out the historical fact that until 1266 the Shetlands, Orkneys, Hebrides, and the Isle of Man did not belong to Scotland at all, but were earldoms of the kingdom of Norway.

So you see that Sutherland was rightly called the South Land, for it was south to the Vikings living in the Orkneys and Shetlands, and in this county we find the Norse names such as *Caithness, Thurso, Wick. Loch Laxford* (*lax* = "salmon," cf. Mod. Ger.), and *Strath Helmsdale*, however, show both Celtic and Norse elements and indicate the admixture of races in that district, and the distribution of the names seems to show that the incoming Norse kept to the coast, while the natives took refuge in the hills and the less cultivated parts.

In the Shetlands almost all the local names are Norse; we have bays such as *Nestvoe, Saxaford, Laxvoe*; the farm names end, as in Norway, in *seter, ster*, and the hills are called *how, hoy*, and *holl*.

The various islands are called by names ending in the Norwegian *a*, "island," as *Sanda* (sand isle), *Stronsa* (stream isle), *Westra* (west isle), while the name *Ronaldsa* seems to point to the fact that this island was colonised by a Viking named Ronald.

You will find that the names of most of the small islands of the Hebrides are Norse, while those on the mainland near by are Celtic, a fact which fits in with what we know of the habits of the sea kings, who used to withdraw to islands off the coast during the winter to begin their raids again in the summer.

When you read next of the Bishop of Sodor and Man, you can connect him with the Hebrides, which the Norwegians called *Sudreyjar* or the Southern Islands. In the eleventh century these islands, together with the Isle of Man, were put under the pastoral care of the Bishop of Trondheim in Norway, but the inhabitants of the Hebrides have long been Presbyterian, and the Bishop of Sodor and Man has rule over them no longer, though the title remains.

In the Isle of Man you will find many Norse names; villages such as *Colby*, *Kirby*, bays such as *Sandwick*, *Soderwick*, while *Snaefell* (snow hill) is purely Norwegian. From the map you can see that the Norse names are chiefly to the south of the island owing to the fact that Earl Goddard of Iceland took the island, and, keeping the more fertile southern district for himself and his followers, left the more barren mountainous portions to the natives—a proceeding usual on the part of invaders.

In the Lake District we find many northern names, as is seen by the frequency of the suffixes *thwaite, force, gill, garth, fell*; *ness* is seen in *Furness, Bowness*; and Icelandic names, geographical and personal, are to be found in this region.

Just as we know that the Northmen must have

had colonies on the spits of land at the mouths of the Stour and the Yare, so we find a Norse settlement on the *Wirral*, the tongue of land between the Dee and the Mersey, for, owing to its isolated position, it would form a very safe retreat with good harbourage on each side of the spit. In this small area very many of the names are Norse, and in the very centre is the village of *Thingwell*, marking the spot where the *Thing*, or local-government assembly of the Northmen, used to meet.

Travelling southward round the coast, we find traces of the Vikings in such names as *Milford*, *Haverford*, *Stack Island*, *Caldy Island*, and *Lundy Island*.

In Ireland the Northmen had several important settlements, the towns of *Dublin*, *Waterford*, *Limerick*, and *Cork* being in their hands, and the Scandinavians in Dublin had their own laws and government right up till the thirteenth century, and their own quarter of the city guarded by gates and walls and called *Oxmanstown* (Osmanstown, the East men's town).

Even from these few examples we can gather that the study of geographical names is full of interest and romance; the last Viking has long since sailed on his last voyage and his history is but scantily written in books, but the names he gave to his haunts and the very words he used have proved vigorous and undying.

# PLACE NAMES

We have confined ourselves to tracing roughly the pathway of the Northmen round the British coast, but it is equally plainly marked through France, Italy, Spain, and other countries of Europe where they penetrated, and, if you go to Venice and examine carefully the marble lions over the entrance to the arsenal, lions which came from the Piraeus at Athens, you will find them deeply scored with runes telling of the capture of the Piraeus by Harold Hardrada, who was killed in the battle of Stamford Bridge after a life full of adventure.

If only those sculptured lions could speak, what stories they could tell!

But we must return to our next conquerors.

If people know no other date in English history, they generally know that the Norman Conquest took place—or rather began—in 1066, but they do not always realise that the Normans who came over with William the Conqueror were Northmen—descendants of the Vikings who had settled in Normandy when their relations came to Britain. They were therefore closely related to the majority of the English nation, though, during their sojourn in France, they had lost many of their old national characteristics, while their language had changed very greatly.

At the time of the Conquest the language spoken in our island was Anglo-Saxon or Early English, and that spoken by the invaders Norman-French; but in spite of the fact that the new-comers became the possessors of most of the land after the battle of Hastings, the map shows comparatively few traces of their influence.

As a matter of fact the Normans were very few compared with the English, and being mostly barons, they did not mix with the people, with whom the former names of places remained unchanged to a large extent. A few of the more obvious French names will come to mind at once, such as *Belvoir Castle* (fine view), *Beaumont* (fine hill), *Montacute Hill*, *Chester-le-Street* (Lat. + Fr. + Lat.), *Beaulieu, Rivaulx* and *Jervaulx Abbeys*, *Gracedieu Abbey* in Leicester, and *Beauchamp*.

Others are *Stoke Mandeville, Ashby-de-la-Zouch, Stoke Pirou, Hurstmonceaux, Hurstpierpoint*, the last two being in Sussex, where William of Normandy landed and where we find the land divided by the *hrepp* (rope) as Rolf the first Viking in Normandy would have divided it, whereas in other parts of the country it was divided into the *hundreds* and *wapentakes* of the Anglo-Saxons and Danes.

In Wales we have Norman French names as *Beaumaris* (fine marsh), *Mold* (mount), *Montgomery, Capel Curig* (capel = chapelle), and in Scotland we find disguised French names as *Maxwell* (Maccusville) and *Somerville*.

But we must leave this fascinating part of the

## PLACE NAMES

subject and pass on to see what a number of our everyday words have a geographical origin; for just as we saw that all local names were once words, so many words were once local names.

First among these let us think of some animals which have been named from the country they came from, and a few very obvious ones will at once come to mind, as *canary, guineafowl, newfoundlands, shetlands, dorkings, arabs, alderneys.*

Others more disguised are *pheasant*, the Phasian bird, from the R. Phasis in Asia Minor, and *tarantula*, a spider found in Taranto, Italy; but *turkeys* did not originally come from Turkey, but from America, and were misnamed owing to the idea that they came from the Levant.

Many articles of food, plants, and flowers have geographical names, as the obvious examples, *swedes, savoys, damsons* (Damascus), *currants* (Corinth), *mocha, cayenne, brazils, cypress*, probably from Cyprus.

Not so easily recognised are *peach* = the Persian fruit (Lat. *persicum*), *cherry* probably from Cerasus on the Black Sea, and *rhubarb*, the root from the banks of the savage River Rha (Volga) which was known as barbarum (savage).

Most wines are named from the place they come from, as *champagne, burgundy, madeira, port* (Oporto), and the same may be said of many fabrics, though now most of these materials are manufactured in

England, France, or Germany and exported to the land of their origin.

*Cashmere* was of course first woven from the wool of the Cashmere sheep, *calico* came originally from Calicut, and *cambric* from Cambrai. How many people who wear *tweed* think of the river, or of the Channel Islands when they wear a *jersey*, or of a village in Norfolk, colonised by Flemings, when they use *worsted* ?

Some miscellaneous words having a geographical origin are *parchment* from Pergamus, where was a great library full of manuscripts ; *lumber* may be from Lombardy, for the Lombards (who settled in Lombard Street) were pawnbrokers and would keep the pawns in a room—the lumber-room. A *tartar*, in the expression " to catch a tartar," is from the fact that the Tartars, inhabitants of Tartary in Asia, were wild and fierce and frequently invaded Eastern Europe in the Middle Ages and their descendants are the Turks of the present day. *Tartar* should be spelt *Tatar*, the first *r* being due to popular etymology which regarded Tartars as being let loose from hell, or Tartarus, as it was called by the Greeks.

A *cannibal* now means any human being who feeds on the flesh of his fellows, but the name was first applied to the natives of the Caribbean Islands, the West Indian word *carib* meaning " brave," for cannibals think that he who eats the heart of a

# PLACE NAMES

warrior will himself become brave. The word was originally spelt *canibal*.

A *milliner* is, strictly speaking, a dealer in goods from Milan; *italics* are so called because their inventor, Aldo Manuzio, was an Italian (circa 1501), while those who *canter* are possibly following, as we have seen, the example of the pilgrims of Chaucer's days who visited the shrine of St. Thomas of Canterbury.

Some places are so named from their size, as in the case of *Majorca* (larger) and *Minorca* (smaller), *Bradford* (broad), *Penmaenmawr* (*mawr* = " great "); while others take their name from their relative position, as *Essex* (the land of the East Saxons), *Westbury*, *Northumberland*, *Ostend* (at east end of the canal); *Pekin* and *Nankin*, north and south courts. *Netherby*, *Deeping*, and *Holloway* are naturally low-lying places, while *Highgate*, *High Barnet* are on rising ground. In every country there are places named from their relative age, as *Newcastle*, *Newton*, *Oldham*, *Nova Zembla*, *Aldburgh*; while others are found in which numerals play a part, as in *Sevenoaks*, *Nine-Elms*, *Zweibrücken* (two bridges), *Punjab* (land of five rivers), *Plynlimmon* (five hills), and in the Rhine valley there are some villages on the sites of Roman stations which take their modern names from the old Latin numerals : *Seguns*, *Tertzen*, *Quarten*, *Quinten*, *Sewes* (secundus, tertius, quartus, quintus, sextus, i.e. second, third, etc.).

Some places gain their name from their characteristic production, as in the case of many mineral springs, shown by the prefix *aix* (Lat. *aqua* = " water"), as *Aix-la-Chapelle*; *Terra del Fuego* is the land of fire; *Hecla* means " cloak " in reference to the pall of smoke over the mountain; *Sandwich* means " sandy bay," while the *Gold Coast* and *Ivory Coast* were suitably named by the early traders.

Animals have frequently given their names to places, as can be noticed in such names as *Beverly* (beaver), *Ely*, once famous for eels in which the island paid its rent; *Hertford* (hart), *Otterbourne*, *Cranbourne* (crane), *Loch Laxford* (*lax* = " salmon "), *Earne* (egle, A.S.).

Of names recalling trees and plants we have *Oakley*, *Elmswell*, *Ashton*, *Bircholt*, *Appleby*, *Sedgemoor*, *Haslemere*, *Saffron Walden* (saffron cultivated there formerly), and *Mount of Olives*.

And so we might go on at any length, finding ever fresh interest in the place names we know so well and yet use with never a thought as to their origin. The true value of every branch of study lies in its *humanity*, and few subjects can be more human than the study of words in whatever form they appear.

# CHAPTER VIII

### PERSONAL NAMES

LET us now ask ourselves with Juliet, "What's in a name?" and perhaps even the brief answer that we shall be able to give to that question will throw some light on the names of ourselves and our friends, for names, like other words, have long and interesting histories.

Everyone has at least two names—his family, sir-, or surname which he inherits from his father, and his first, Christian, or baptismal name which is given him by his parents. Of course the first name is now generally chosen without any reference to its real meaning, though parents often call a child after some ancestor or celebrity, or by some name suggested by its birthday; but family names are permanent and can be traced back to some common ancestor.

Personal names were bestowed in the first instance for the purpose of distinguishing one person from another or to mark some special characteristic in the owner, and were not at first permanent or hereditary; but in the thirteenth and fourteenth centuries the population increased so rapidly in Europe generally that they were used much more frequently and gradually became general and at length compulsory. Before the compulsory stage was reached it had become a mark of gentle birth to have two names, so that it was looked upon as a disgrace to have only one.

You will notice that among the Hebrews there were no family names; a man was known as the son of his father and as a member of a tribe, as in the case of *Joshua, the son of Nun*; *Saul, the son of Kish*; *Jehu, the son of Nimshi*, and this custom prevailed largely among them through the Middle Ages. In the beginning of the nineteenth century, however, all the Jews in Austria, Prussia, and Bavaria were compelled to take a surname, which accounts for the fact that many Jews of to-day have family names corresponding to the names of towns or other places. Casting about for some suitable name to adopt, they frequently took that of the place in which they lived, as in the case of *London, Kopenhagen, Cassel, Speyer*. Sometimes they took the name of an animal and so appear as *Löwe* (lion), *Hirsch* (stag), or a purely fanciful name as *Rosenberg* (rose-mountain), or merely added *son* to their father's name, as *Samuelson, Jacobson*, now generally shortened to *Samuels* and *Jacobs*.

Among the Anglo-Saxons, too, a man was known

as the son of his father, though we also have the forms *Edward the Confessor*, *Edmund Ironsides*, *Harold Harefoot*. In the northern counties to-day we find people frequently known as the son or daughter of their father or mother, though, of course, they possess surnames; while in Iceland surnames do not exist at all and a man appears only as *Eric, the son of Jan*, and so on.

The origin of names such as Williamson, Richardson, Johnson, is, of course, quite easy to see, and we often find the shortened forms Williams, Richards, Johns, and Wills.

Among the Anglo-Saxons the suffix *ing* was used to denote *son*, as in *Edmunding*, the son of Edmund, *Wulfing*, the son of Wulf; while the prefixes *Mac*, *Mc* in Scotland, *M'* and *O'* in Ireland, *Fitz* (fr. *filz*, *fils*) in France, had the same meaning, though in Scotland and Ireland the prefix showed membership in a tribe or clan, as well as actual sonship.

We have not many surnames which carry us back to Anglo-Saxon times, and those we have are a good deal disguised; a few examples are, Harman (*hereman* = " army man "), Herbert (*here-beorht* = " army-bright "), Baldwin (*beald* = " bold "), Kemp (*cempa* = " messenger ").

Just as words have come to us from all countries and have often changed much in their journeys, so it is with names, and it is in many cases difficult, if not impossible, to trace their origin. We may, however, perhaps classify surnames into five groups according to their origin.

(1) In the first group we may put all those derived from the name of a place, often the home of some ancient family, as *Essex, Cheshire, Cornwallis* (Cornwall), *Bristow* (Bristol). Often we find simply the word for some natural feature, as *Hall, Wood, Green, Lea, Hill, Shaw, Petch* (peak); or that compounded with a personal name, as in *Fothergill, Gaskell* (*gill* and *kell* = Sc. for " ravine"). Sometimes we find a geographical name coupled with a preposition, as in *Atwood, Underhill, Attenborough, Surtees*, the last being a compound of the French preposition *sur* and the name of an English river.

It will be found that by far the greater number of personal names with a geographical origin come from villages or small country towns, for movement has always been from the provinces to large centres, and a countryman would be called *John of Reading* to distinguish him from John of Newton and all the other Johns, and later, the preposition having dropped, he would be plain John Reading.

Thus you will find *Scott* as an English name, *English* as a Scotch name, and *German* or *French* as an English name, for it was only when a man travelled to another country that there was any need to emphasise his nationality.

As a result of the Norman Conquest and our frequent wars with France all through the Middle Ages, we have many surnames of French origin, such as *Bullen* and *Boleyn* (Boulogne), *Cullen* (Cologne), *Challis* (Calais), *Bruce* (Brieux), *Boswell* (Bosville), *Gascoigne* (Gascony), *Danvers* (d'Anvers = Antwerp), while *Pollack, Pollock,* and its variants mean " the Pole," of which Shakespeare speaks in *Hamlet* IV, 4 when he says, " Why then the Polack never will defend it," and speaks of " the sledded Polacks on the ice " in the same play.

(2) The second class of surnames contains those that show the trade, profession, or other occupation of the first person who adopted that name for his family. Of course many people are now called *Smith* who have nothing to do with a forge, but their common ancestors of centuries back followed that calling, which was most necessary in the days when war was always in the air and all fighting men wore armour.

Names derived from occupations are often much disguised in their present form and frequently are survivals of callings which no one now follows. For instance, the *chapman*, a dealer or merchant, was once a familiar figure in English society, who has left many descendants, and we still speak of *chopping* ( = chapping) and *changing*, though we do not mean by it " buying and selling " as he did; while our adjective *cheap* was originally a noun meaning "a market," and remains in the names *Cheapside* (*Chepeside*) and *Chipping Norton* and its relations.

The old English grocer (Fr. *engros, engrosser*, a man who bought wholesale) was called a *spicer*, a word which has survived as a surname, though in other uses it has been supplanted by the French equivalent. *Farrar* is from "farrier" and *Poyser* from "the poiser" or scale-maker (Fr. *poises*).

You will perhaps be surprised to find what a number of surnames have come to us from the cloth trade. To begin with there was the *packer*, who fastened the bales of wool and saw that each was of a certain weight; then came the *stapler* (*Staples* and *Staple*), who sorted the wool, while the *comber* combed it and the *spinner* spun it. The *warper* arranged the thread for the *weaver* (*Webster, Webber, Webb*), who wove it and passed it on to the *carder*, who sent it to the *fuller*, who washed it and was sometimes called a *walker*. It was then the turn of the *dyer*, of the *tenter*, who stretched it, and of the *lister*, who was a counter. If the stuff in question was linen it had to be bleached by the *tucker* or *fuller*, and if woollen the nap was brought up by the *tozer* or *towzer* by means of teazles. The English for tailor (Taylor) was *shaper*; the man who put on lace or braid was a *trimmer*, and, in the days of tags or points, there was a *pointer*.

The trades of arrow-making have also given us a

good number of surnames, such as *Arrowsmith, Setter, Tipper, Fletcher* (Fr. *flêche*), *Shafter, Bowyer,* and *Bolter,* the last being the man who made the bolts for the cross-bows.

The name *Falconer* carries us back to the days when hawking was a royal sport and the charge of the hawks and falcons an honourable position; while *Todhunter* (foxhunter) reminds us of the times when twelve pence (worth more than a shilling then) was paid for every fox killed. A *barker* prepared bark for tanning, while *Forester, Foster, Forster* are the descendants of an ancestor whose occupation was forestry.

In former days a *bin* was called an *ark,* so that we get the name *Arkwright* as we have wheelwright, while Chaucer's ancestors made stockings, for the name is from the French *chaucier* = " a hosier." In French there is generally a feminine form for the follower of any special trade and occupation, as we learn from the French exercise book; this form occurs very seldom in English, but we have one example in Labouchere = "the butcheress."

*Ward* ( = guard or keeper) gives us the compounds *Hayward* (hedge guard) and *Hereward* (army guard); while the suffix *herd* ( = herdsman) gives *Shepherd, Calvert* (calf-herd), *Stoddart* ( = Stot-herd, i.e. bullock-herd), while hog-herd appears in two forms, *Hoggart* and *Hogarth.*

(3) Among all peoples it is the custom to bestow nicknames, which are generally suggested by some characteristic of habit or appearance, and, in the first instance, are not always complimentary. Many surnames have come into existence in this way and have equivalents in other languages. Thus we have *Drinkwater* (Boileau), *Merryweather* (Bontemps), *Armstrong* (Fortinbras), while popular corruptions of French give us such names as *Bonner* (débonnaire), *Blunt* (blond), *Grant* (grand).

We have as colour names *Black*, *White*, *Brown*, *Grey* (all colours of hair), but not red, perhaps because we seem to have adopted in its place the French *roux*, *rouge*, *Rousseau*, which have given us *Rouse*, *Rudge*, and *Russell*, or the northern form *Reid*, and its variants *Reed* and *Read*. The good old English name of *Fairfax* contains the Anglo-Saxon word *feax*, "hair."

Animals have in many cases given their name to people, perhaps on account of some resemblance in feature or character, perhaps from some incident in the person's history that was connected with that animal. Examples of this class of name are *Lamb*, *Rook*, *Brock* (badger), *Hogg*; while from trees, for the same reason probably, we get *Rowntree* (rowan), *Hollins* (holly), *Lyndhurst* (lime).

(4) Many surnames are merely baptismal names disguised, as *Cobbett* (Cuthbert), *Hibbert* (Hubert),

*Jessop* (Joseph), while some have the diminutive suffix, as *Atkin* (Adam), *Larkin* (Lawrence), *Perkin* (Peter), *Huggin, Hewlett, Hutchin,* and *Howett* (Hugh), and *Gilpin* (Gilbert). *Philpot* is from Philip, *Mayhew* from Matthew; while Robert gives us *Robson, Dobson, Hobson*; and Richard, *Dickson, Dickins, Hickson,* and *Dickers.*

Baptismal names that help to form surnames often show what were the most popular names in early times, and many of these were taken from the Bible or from the lives and legends of the saints which people would know from the mystery and miracle plays. The mass of the population could not read, but they watched or took part in the plays, and the name of any particular character would readily become attached to the person who had taken that part. The most usual names of this class seem to have been those of the apostles, Old Testament characters such as David (*Davidson, Davison, Davies, Davis*), Job (*Jobson, Jobling, Jupp, Chubb*), Adam (*Adams, Adamson, Adkin, Adcock, Addison, Atkinson*), Moses (*Moss*), while Stephen gives *Stephenson, Stephens, Stevens, Stevenson.*

Considering the fact that S. George was the patron saint of England and King Arthur the hero of chivalry and legend, their names seem to have been seldom bestowed, but Thomas à Becket and both the saints named John were responsible for many namesakes.

Richard the Lion Heart and Robin Hood were the cause of the popularity of their respective names, the frequent bestowal of which perhaps giving rise to the nursery rhyme of "Richard and Robert were two pretty men."

In some ages and countries it has been the custom to inherit the name from the mother instead of the father, which fact accounts for such names as *Anson* (Ann), *Eames, Empson* (Emma), *Mallinson, Marriott, Maxon* (Mary), *Tillet, Tillotson* (Mathilda).

The distribution of family names is a subject full of interest, and if you examined lists of names occurring in certain districts you would be struck by the frequency with which certain names are found in some parts and hardly at all in others. Of course in estimating such distribution one must allow for migration and immigration, but, to avoid the effect of this interchange as far as possible it is best to consider the yeoman class, for they, as farmers, are the most stationary.

You will find that Cornwall and Lancashire are the two counties having the largest number of surnames peculiar to that country, for they head the list with 168 and 137 respectively; then comes Cornwall with 134, while Middlesex has only two, which you may like to know—they are *Ewer* and *Woodland*.

These facts are what we should expect, for the population of the two western counties is likely to be more stationary and less mixed than that of Middlesex with its city of London.

On looking into this matter of the distribution of surnames you will find some interesting and peculiar facts, a few of which we will notice; if you care to study the matter very fully you cannot do better than consult *The Homes of Family Names in Great Britain*, by H. B. Guppy.

You will find that whereas the surname Grey (Gray) occurs frequently all along the eastern coast of England from Northumberland to Kent, and then again in Hampshire and Dorset, it seems never to have taken up its home in Sussex. In North Durham we get the spelling *Grey*, while *Greyson* is found only in Yorkshire, and *Grey* is frequent in Kent. The form *Gray* is found in Lincoln, once in Oxford and again in Bucks, Cambridge, and neighbouring counties.

By saying that a name does not occur in a certain county, we mean that it does not appear as a native name in any old records; if it occurs there at all it is merely as the result of immigration.

In this question of distribution you will find that *trade* names are very important. For instance, in connection with the cloth industry you will notice the following facts.

Names connected with weaving, as *Webb*, *Webber*, *Webster*, are commonest south of the Wash, especially in Somerset, Wilts, and Hants; *Webbers* are found in Devon, *Weavers* in Worcester and Gloucester, while north of the Wash and the Dee we find the feminine form *Webster*.

*Tucker* (the synonym of *Fuller*) is met with especially in Devon and Somerset, *Fuller* in the east and south-east, Sussex, Kent, and Norfolk, while *Walker* occurs in the rest of England generally, but especially in Derby, Notts, and Yorks.

As a few examples of celebrated names native to certain counties we may mention *Thackeray, Shackleton, Jowett*, and *Lodge,* all peculiar to Yorkshire; *Darwin* native to Notts; *Wren, Nightingale, Hemans* to Sussex.

Just as many baptismal and family names (or perhaps we might say most or even all) began as common nouns or adjectives (*Margaret* = a pearl, *Peter* = a rock, *Clara* = famous, and so on), so many proper names have returned again to their former state and appear as common nouns.

Some you will recognise at once, others are more or less disguised.

Flowers, for instance, and scientific terms often have personal names, as *dahlia* (Dahl), *camellia* (Camel), *fuchsia* (Fuchs), all named from their first grower; and scientific terms are *volt, mesmerise.* *Hansom* cabs were so named from their inventor Mr. Hansom; policemen are called *bobbies* from Sir Robert Peel, who first organised them in place of the old watchmen or Charlies; and *macadam* pavement is so called from Mr. Macadam.

The *atlas* used in school is named after Atlas who bore the world on his shoulders; *March* is the month of Mars, *July* the month of Julius Caesar, *August* that of Augustus Caesar.

We remember our heathen forefathers and their gods every time we mention the days of the week, for *Wednesday* is Woden's day; *Thursday*, Thor's day; *Friday*, the day of the goddess Freya.

The verb *tantalise* reminds us of Tantalus, who was condemned to stand for ever in water that receded whenever he tried to quench his burning thirst, and before whose longing eyes luscious fruits hung ever just out of reach.

The *phaeton* we drive in is the modern equivalent of the chariot of the Sun, which Phaeton drove to his destruction; a *volcano* sends up smoke and fire from the forges of Vulcan, the god of fire; while *panic*, originally an adjective applied to the terror inspired by Pan the goat-legged god of the woods, is now a noun.

A man who speaks very loudly may be said to have a *stentorian* voice, because among the Greeks in the Trojan war was a herald, Stentor, who could shout as loud as fifty men; a task that is almost impossible is called *herculean* from the twelve labours of Hercules; and when we say some one *meandered* along we are unconsciously referring to a slow-flowing and winding stream of Asia Minor, the Maeander.

A *quixotic* person is really a follower of Don Quixote, the hero of Cervantes, while Wellington has given his name to high boots, Napoleon to a French coin, and Gladstone to a bag.

The little stormy *petrel* that floats calmly on the waves of the stormiest sea is so called after S. Peter who walked on the water, the German name for this bird being *Peters Vogel*, Peter's bird.

You would hardly think at first sight that the word *tawdry* had anything to do with a saint, but it is a corruption of S. Audrey, sometimes called S. Etheldreda. In olden times on her feast-day, October 17, a fair used to be held in country towns and villages, where cheap finery was sold at the stalls and called S. Audrey's finery; gradually the last word dropped out and the saint's name was corrupted into the modern adjective.

Thus you see that personal names form a real part of our language, for by their means our tongue grows yearly, with such terms as *Zeppelin*, and will ever continue to grow.

# CHAPTER IX

### NATIONAL CHARACTER AND LANGUAGE

IN this chapter we shall try to show that the characteristics peculiar to a nation are reflected in their language, and that languages, as well as people, have character.

Just as you can tell a great deal about a man from the style of his written work—the sort of letter he writes, the kind of words and expressions he uses, the turn of his sentences, and the class of illustration which seems to appeal to him—so we can see in a people's language and literature the outstanding features of its national character.

We know that climate has a great effect on speech and the organs of speech—those people who live in warm, sunny lands, where Nature is an indulgent mother, speak a language that is soft and flexible, are fond of vowel sounds and avoid consonants and anything harsh. We know too, on the other hand, that in those countries where Nature is a stern taskmistress, where the climate is inhospitable and life is largely a struggle, the people speak languages that harmonise with their surroundings—the harshness of

Nature is reflected in the hard consonants with which these tongues bristle.

The language of the mountains is different from that of the plain, for the life of each creates different needs; the speech of the city is different from that of the village, and the idea of a Viking speaking the soft syllables of southern Italy is at once absurd. A Scotsman or an Irishman can be distinguished from an Englishman, not only by a difference of accent, but by a use of slightly different forms in addition to the difference of intonation; and an example still more noticeable is that of the American and Colonial "twang," which foreigners acquire unconsciously after even a short residence in the country, while their vocabulary changes considerably in a very little while.

If, then, variations and changes such as these can be noted, should we not expect to find that during the course of ages the mother tongues of the various peoples of the world have taken to themselves the peculiarities and characteristics of the nations, and, though having many things in common, possess each an individuality?

A national language is a national heritage, a national chronicle. Schlegel says: "A nation whose language becomes rude and barbarous must be on the brink of barbarism in regard to everything else. A nation which allows her language to go to ruin is parting with the last half of her intellectual independence and testifies her willingness to cease to exist " (*History of Literature*, Lecture 10).

You will notice, I think, that the interjections of a nation are very characteristic and are among the last bits of a language to be acquired by a foreigner, and the special intonation with which these exclamations are uttered is even more characteristic, being very obscure and hard to catch and imitate.

Among the nations of the East there is a certain sadness of intonation, an almost wailing note as of the minor key which is in all their music and in that of savage tribes; the interjections of the southern countries, such as Italy and Spain, incline to vowels, while those of the Northern Teutonic peoples show a preference for consonants.

This Eastern note of sadness is noticeable among the Greeks, with whom there is a sort of suppressed sob in everything, an autumn wind sighing in the spring. Essentially poets and philosophers as they were, their language is wonderfully rich and expressive and suited to convey all the workings of the master minds of the world.

The language of Italy is exactly framed to express the character of its people—soft and flexible, sweeter and more graceful than Latin, it has been accepted on all sides as a fitting medium for the expression of all the art and poetry and romance associated with Italy,

In Spanish, with its dignified prose, we find a language admirably suited for serious narrative, combined with an ingenious taste for wit, great richness of expression, grace, and poetry—a tongue well suited to the dignity of the proud Spanish don and yet having something in common with the gayer side of romantic adventures and midnight serenades.

Are not the French the courtiers *par excellence*, and is not theirs the language of diplomacy? But they are more than courtiers, they are philosophers, and, though very practical, are idealists too; close observers of men and morals, they are gifted with a power of analysis and clearness of thought which their language enables them to express better, perhaps, than any other people.

But to pass from generalisations, let us look a little more closely at a few languages and see if from them we can gather any idea of the character of the people who use them as their mother tongue, for, of course, as a result of conquest or migration, many peoples to-day speak a tongue which is really foreign to them.

Let us in this case go back to the beginning, or as near the beginning as possible, and by that I mean, let us consider the people who spoke the early Mother Tongue, the Indo-European language of which we spoke in the first chapter, and, by dealing with the words we possess to-day which are descended from that language, let us try to form some idea of our forefathers of perhaps 3,000 years ago and probably much earlier.

Now we do not possess anything written in this early Mother Tongue and so do not actually know what it was. How then can we say we are going to tell something of the character of the people from the language they spoke ? We do so by starting with languages we do know, and, guided by rules, according to which words and letters always change quite regularly in passing from one language to another, we trace back words to the form they wore in the early Mother Tongue.

You will remember from our first chapter that the Old Persian (Zend) and the Old Indian (Sanskrit) languages were the Asiatic daughters of the Mother Tongue, while in Europe we have Greek, the Romance family, and the Teutonic group among others.

Now, to get any knowledge of the Mother Tongue, we must study carefully all her descendants, and when we find a word that appears, though often under a disguise, in all or nearly all these languages, we conclude that it was a word that the early race knew when it was still one and undivided in its early home, and that, therefore, it was one of the words of the Indo-European speech.

You will realise at once what a long and difficult task this must have been, but scholars have worked devotedly, with the result that we can gather a very good idea of the life and character of our early ancestors from the words traced back thus to their early home; so that, as already said, words have astonishing vitality, and live on long after the men who used them first have passed away, and not only live, but weave romances for us of the early history of our race.

The first fact that seems very clear about this early race, whom we will call Aryans for want of a better short name, is that they were a pastoral people; some primitive tribes are still in this stage of existence, but the conclusion is supported, in this case, by the evidence of language.

The Aryans might have been an agricultural people, a stage next to that of the pastoral life, but we conclude that they were not so advanced and that for many reasons.

Firstly, there are in the daughter languages many words common to all relating to cows and the care of cattle, and very few relating to agriculture—not enough to lead us to think that sowing and reaping and ploughing—agricultural pursuits—were carried on more than occasionally as the tribes camped for a time in their wanderings in search of pasture.

Cows there were in plenty, also oxen, sheep, and goats, for these animals could be driven in herds from place to place; but of other animals, except the wild horse and boar, there seems little trace, nor of poultry, which would be difficult to keep safe from foes without more enclosures and shelters than a nomad (wandering) people would be likely to put up.

The dog, however, was already the friend of man and his name is found in all the daughter languages.

All the wealth of the Aryans consisted in cattle, in support of which we may remember that the word in Sanskrit for " king " (*gopa*) originally meant " a cowherd," " the owner of a cow-pen," and so came to mean " the richest man in the tribe," therefore " the chief."

The Sanskrit word for " assembly " or " tribe " came originally from the word for an enclosure for cows, and then gradually grew to mean " the herd inside " and then " the tribe," while the word used in the Vedas for " warrior " really means " a striver for cows," showing clearly that the wealth of the people was measured by cattle.

In all the daughter languages we get further proof of this fact by finding that the word from which " money " comes originally meant " cattle," or " that which has been tied up," cf. Lat. *pecus* (a herd), *pecunia* (money); Eng. *fee*, A.S. *feoh* (cattle or property), Ger. *vieh* (cattle), all of which are varying forms of the same word. Strangely enough, too, we can still speak of money being " tied up."

In Homer, who tells of very early Greek times,

we find things valued by oxen—Glaucus was worth 100 oxen; one female slave was worth 20; another, poor thing, was valued at 4 only!

Another interesting fact is that the only words for colours that belong to all the Aryan languages are those applicable to cattle, as red and white, while blue and green, etc., crept in after the races separated.

The idea that the undivided Aryans had not reached the agricultural stage of existence gains support from the fact that there is no word for "plough" common to all the daughter languages, nor for autumn, the time for ingathering, though there is one for winter, the time when the herds would have to be driven in, and another for summer, the season when the cows could be driven to pasture. We may notice here that autumn was the last season to be named, because by the time a people had reached the stage of a regular ingathering of crops they had developed some way beyond a merely pastoral existence.

Still the fact that the English word *grist* = " grain," has relations in all the related languages, proves that some sort of grain was known to the undivided Aryans —perhaps it was wild barley; we cannot tell.

Flax they knew, too, for there are words for weaving, and they made rough garments by sewing together skins and they seem to have plaited the fibres of certain plants into mats,

# NATIONALITY AND LANGUAGE 201

Of weapons they seem to have had bows of yew and spears of ash and shields of twisted osier.

Their chief food was probably cooked flesh—often the wild boar and horse—for there is a common word " to cook " and another for " knead," so that they had some form of bread, and of course milk, though butter and cheese were apparently not known till after the separation of the peoples.

The question as to whether the undivided Aryan knew the sea is not definitely settled; there is a common word for " mere " (Lat. *mare*, Fr. *mer*), but there is no word for " fish," which, one would have thought, must have been a common article of food for any primitive people living near a river or sea; all the words, too, connected with fishing, " net," " line," " hook," " bait," are different in Greek and Latin and the allied languages.

In support of the idea that the Aryans did not eat fish, it has been urged that the Lake Dwellers of Switzerland—(a primitive people who lived in huts built on wooden piles in the Swiss lakes, and who were probably at a stage of development something similar to the Aryans)—did not eat fish, as no such remains have been found among the relics that have been discovered, though one would have thought fish the one food they would have consumed.

Water of some kind, however, the Aryans must have known, as they had words for " to row " and for "rudder" (originally an oar or paddle), which fact shows that they had some sort of rough boat or canoe, dug out with a stone hatchet or burnt by fire from the trunk of a tree, for the word for "boat" in all the daughter languages is related to the word for "tree."

The Aryans certainly used wooden wagons drawn by oxen, for there are common words for "to drive," "axle," "wheel," "yoke," all connected with the word for "wood," and it is otherwise unlikely that any metal would be used, for there is only one word for "ore" or "metal," by which is probably meant "copper," that being the metal generally known to primitive people.

That the Aryans lived sometimes (probably in winter) in huts of some kind seems proved by the fact that they had words for "roof," "door," and "doorposts," though the dwellings were probably rude huts of sticks, thatched with twigs and leaves.

They evidently had some idea of family life, for they had words for the various relationships, though some of them have been lost in the daughter languages.

The words "cough," "wound," "heal," show some idea of the medical art, and we know that they made from honey a drink something like the mead drunk by our Anglo-Saxon forefathers.

They could count up to a hundred, as the word

for that number is common to all the daughter languages, and that they used their fingers as the basis of counting is shown by the fact that the word "five" originally meant "hand"; they could not count up to a thousand, for the word for that number is different in all Aryan tongues. Their time was measured by the moon, which was called "the measurer."

Of the religion of these early people we know practically nothing—the word for "idol" is not common to all the Aryan languages and we can deduce very little; but it seems that they worshipped the sun and moon and the forces of nature—night and stars, dew and snow and wind, thunder, fire, and east are all early words and the Aryans seem to have regarded the sky as a sort of god.

Ancestor worship may have prevailed among them as it does among so many primitive peoples and can be traced in many of the early daughter languages; and a word for "tree," which sometimes means "oak" (though the various nations seem to have applied it indiscriminately to different trees), and the frequency of a word meaning "acorn," seem to point to the fact that this nut was an ordinary article of food and that the oak was connected with the sky or thunder god as it was among the ancient Druids.

The result of this tracing back of words, then, is

that we have a very fair idea of the life of our early ancestors.

They were a pastoral people, driving their cattle from place to place in the summer, living in rude huts in the winter, feeding on flesh, milk, and vegetables and wearing rough garments of skins.

Most of the words that have come down to us are homely terms, and perhaps not in themselves romantic; but when we think that by their means and by their undying spirit the abyss of ages is bridged, so that we can picture to ourselves the life of our early ancestors, we look with a sort of wonder at these words which have lived on to tell us of a people whose history would otherwise be a blank.

We have said above that the language we have been trying to trace out was that of the whole Aryan or Indo-European race before it split up and travelled, in groups, to different parts of the continents of Europe and Asia, and it would be very interesting to follow each migration and see how it affected the language, for we can easily understand that for the new ideas suggested by strange lands, fresh words would have to be found or borrowed from the people already settled there.

We have not space to do this in detail, but a few of these changes may be mentioned.

We gather that the undivided Aryans lived in

some rather treeless plain and that the European branch made its way to a country of forests, for in the languages of this branch we soon find many words for trees and birds, as *beech, hazel, elm, throstle, starling, finch,* while the appearance of such words as *mow, corn, furrow, bean, meal* and *ear* (of corn), shows that they were giving themselves to agriculture.

In the early nomadic days, it had probably not been necessary to till the land, and so it had never been done, but now that the Aryans had migrated to a land of forests, scanty pasture, and swamps, they had to labour on the land or die of hunger.

Now also they seem to have come in contact with the sea, for we meet with words for " fish," though it is noticeable that this is not the case with all branches—the word for " sea " does not appear in the early Slavonic language for some time.

Among the Teutonic branch agriculture seems to have developed very widely, and we soon find many additions to the language in the names of birds and beasts and farming terms, while such words as *bowl, brew, broth, dough, loaf, hat, comb, house,* and *home* show the increase in civilisation, and *borough, king,* and *earl,* though not bearing the modern exalted meaning, show advance in social life and organisation.

The beginnings of trade appear in the words *cheap*

(originally a verb = " to barter," for money had not yet appeared), *worth, ware, buy,* and the Northman's love of the sea is shown by terms such as *sea, island, flood, cliff, ship, steer, sail, shower, storm, hail, gull,* and *whale* ( = any large fish).

As throwing some light on the early life of our Teutonic ancestors, look for a moment at a few words that come to us from them, though the meaning has changed with the passage of centuries and the march of civilisation.

Our word *fear* probably goes back to the same Aryan root as *to fare,* meaning " to travel," an adventure which in those days would be full of dangers from wild beasts ; *weary* belongs to a verb meaning " to tramp over wet grounds and moors," and, with the word *learn* = " to follow out a track," gives us a vivid picture of the conditions of travel in those early times.

The German word *Ernte* (harvest) is of the same family as our word " to earn," which comes from one meaning " field labour," and the word *gain,* though it came to us directly from French, goes back originally to a Teutonic word meaning " to hunt or fish or forage " and also " to pasture."

*Dear* originally meant " free " and was therefore used of those who were related to the head of the family, in contradistinction to those who were slaves, and *to bless* meant " to sprinkle with blood in a sacrifice," showing that the ritual use of blood was customary, as is so often the case in early forms of religion.

While our Teutonic ancestors were developing an agricultural life, the southern branches of the Indo-European family were settling along the shores of the Mediterranean, where they came into contact with the civilisation of Egypt and the East.

Here they learnt the arts of building in stone, of mining, and of navigation and the beginnings of art, writing, and mathematics, so that their language developed on quite different lines from those followed by their Teutonic brethren.

And now let us look a little more closely at the language which developed in Rome and see if we can tell from it anything of the character of the people, who, on the decline of Greece, became the masters of the then known world, and I think we shall find that the special characteristics of the Roman nation are very clearly reflected in their language.

Whereas the Greeks were a nation of poets, of thinkers and theorists, to whom *mind* was everything and whose typical word was *logoi* = " words," "thoughts," or "reason," the Romans were essentially practical, a nation of soldiers and statesmen and law-makers, whose word was *res* = " deeds," and whose attitude of mind was one of unruffled good sense and utilitarianism.

The three chief characteristic virtues of the Roman were *pietas* (obedience), *fides* (truthfulness), and *industria* (industry). Aeneas, the national hero, was always *pius Aeneas* = "dutiful Aeneas," and the typical story of him is that which tells how he carried his old father, Anchises, on his shoulders when escaping from the flaming city of Troy.

Obedience to the gods, to his parents, to his superior officer, to military law, and to the State, was instilled into the Roman youth from his earliest years, and Roman history is full of stories of supreme devotion to duty on the part of the inhabitants of the Eternal City.

Not less dear to the Roman was the virtue of *fides* (good faith, honesty), and in the *Aeneid* we read of *fidus Achates* = "faithful, staunch, or trusty Achates," the friend of Aeneas, whose name has thus come down to us as a synonym for staunchness and a proof of the value that the Romans set on this virtue.

Added to these two virtues was that of industry, of a whole-hearted concentration on the work in hand which helped to make the Romans the masters of their world.

The Roman was a serious fellow as a rule, grave, sedate, and responsible—his great virtue, apart from the three mentioned above, being *gravitas* (seriousness or dignity, dependableness), a virtue which, I think, Horace had in mind perhaps when, in answer to his

PLATE X—THE RUTHWELL CROSS.

own question "who is the good man?" (which term to a Roman always meant "a good citizen") he says "he who observes the decrees of the Senate and keeps both the moral and the civil law; he who is the arbitrator in many and serious cases; who is trusted as a surety and by whose testimony causes are safe" (Ep. I. 16).

The Roman, too, loved money and all it could buy; in fact, we may say that to the Roman of the time of Augustus money was the all-important thing, and to express it he had many words. *Pecunia* meant "a sum of money" as opposed to property and never meant "pieces of money"; *argentum* and *aes* meant "silver and copper coined"; *nummus* was the single coin and *moneta* was the poetic word; *res familiaris* or *opes* meant "fortune," "wealth," *pretium* meant "the price," and there are many words to express varying degrees of wealth and poverty.

This love of money is shown by the frequent remonstrances of the humorous philosopher-poet, Horace, against the vice of *avaritia*, that is, "the habit of taking money as the standard in everything," and he repeatedly tells us that the cry of exchange and market is "Get rich! get rich! honestly if you can, but if not, by any means possible."

This love of money and worldly goods is shown in the fact that the Romans, who had no native word for "to think," supplied this want in two cases by words connected with the idea of money—namely, *reor* connected with *res* (property) and *aestimo*, from *aes* meaning really "I reckon the value." The other two words for "to think" were *arbitror*, "I pass a verdict on," and *puto*, "I clean or prune."

In fact, as we have said before, the Romans were not thinkers—they disliked abstract ideas and seldom used them as the subject of a sentence; an abstract noun, in Latin, being found most frequently in an oblique case.

Added to this love of money was a great liking for display; a mania for building was widespread in Rome during the early Empire and we find metaphors borrowed from building very frequently used by writers of the time. This love of display is shown in the magnificent and costly banquets often given in Rome on which enormous sums of money were spent; while the frequent references to, and metaphors borrowed from, the kitchen and cooking show that the Roman thought a great deal of eating and drinking, the subject being often discussed in detail, with what seems to us a want of even ordinary good manners and reticence.

You may be surprised to find that, splendid soldiers as they were, the Romans had no word for our idea of *courage* or *daring*—the nearest approach was *audacia*, which has almost the meaning of "foolhardiness" and was looked upon rather as a vice than as a virtue.

The great qualification for a Roman soldier, apart from obedience, was *fortitudo*, "endurance," which is akin to the verb *fero*, "I bear," and has nothing active in its meaning as "courage" has to our minds.

Though the Roman army was so well developed, the navy was almost neglected until the time of Agrippa, who died 12 B.C., and the Roman did not love the sea with the passionate feeling that is typical of the Englishman. Moreover, there is no native Latin word for "sea," though of course there are many paraphrases for it, as, for example, *mare*, which was generally used, but originally meant "the shining thing"; *aequor* meant "the equal thing," and *altum* corresponds to our "mighty deep"—other names, as *Oceanus*, being borrowings from the Greek.

If the Romans knew and cared little about the sea, we are not surprised to find that, as to the Jews of old, it was a source of fear and dread to them. In Latin literature we frequently find references to the dangers of the deep, the hardships of a sailor's life, the great recklessness of those who tempt the hungry waters and go down to the sea in ships; and Horace says that the people of his time admire the hardihood of the merchant who, driven by the greed for gold and the fear of poverty, braves all these dangers and sails to the farthest Indies in pursuit of wealth.

As an exception to this fear and dread of the sea, we notice the apparent delight that the poet Catullus takes in it—in a poem of his about his yacht he seems really to love the sea, and the salt breezes seem to blow through the verse in a manner very unusual among Latin writers.

That the Roman, brave as he was, knew fear and superstitious dread is very plain from the stories of omens and warnings of which Livy is full, and from the great number of words that we find in Latin to express all varieties of fear. Some such are *metus* and *timor* meaning " fear as a weakness "; *verecundia*, " the fear of what is wrong "; *terror*, " sudden fright "; *pavor*, " alarm "; *trepidatio*, " trembling "; *horror*, " fear that makes your hair stand on end "; *formido*, " shrinking fear "; *timiditas*, " fearfulness "; *ignavia*, meaning " cowardice."

We have said that, compared with the Greeks, the Romans were practical and material in their outlook, which probably accounts for the fact that they have no word for *imagination*, just as they have no word for *history*, to express which they use the term *res gestae* = " things done," therefore " deeds," which were to them more important than words.

In like manner, apart from the one word *carmen*, the Romans had no name for a *poem*, and all their

# NATIONALITY AND LANGUAGE

poetic forms, like their gods and goddesses, were borrowed from Greece.

As in poetry, so in music, the Romans borrowed from the Greeks, their only word for a stringed instrument being *fides* (Gk.), a sort of lute; and though they have many words for *noise* and *wind instruments*, they have none for *music*, and rightly so, for, though they loved noise—the harsh blare of trumpets (*tuba*) and the sound of the horn (*cornu*), they used the same word, *cano*, for the singing of a woman and the crowing of a cock—and their only idea of music can truthfully be called " noise."

The Roman eye, however, was apparently more sensitive than the ear, for, though a preference is shown for the more showy colours, as yellow and red, the Latin language abounds in colour adjectives, while in the poets one meets with frequent word-pictures, vivid if rather conventional, and tinged with the practicability of the Romans, who saw in a grove of trees timber for building, not the beauty of the leaves, in a garden a place for growing herbs and fruits to eat, and in a vineyard the opportunity for producing wine.

As an example of the variety of colour adjectives in Latin, look at the following list of words to express the varying degrees of whiteness:

*Albus*, " a dull white," as opposed to *ater*, " a dull black "; *candidus*, " shining white," as opposed to *niger*, " glossy black " ; our word *candidate* really means " one who wears white robes," as Roman candidates for office wore white robes. Then we have *canus*, " silvery white," " hoary," as of hair ; *albidus*, *subalbidus*, " whitish " ; *purus*, " unstained " ; *niveus*, " white as snow " ; *lacteus*, " white as milk."

Yellow is another colour apparently beloved of the Romans, for note the varied shades shown in the following :

*Gilbus* (cf. Ger. *gelb*) or *gilvus*, " honey-coloured " ; *flavus*, *flaveus*, " golden yellow " ; *fulvus*, " auburn," " reddish yellow " ; *luridus*, " pale yellow," *luteus*, " orange-yellow " ; *galbanus*, " greenish yellow " ; *cadaverosus*, " yellow as a corpse " ; *ravus*, " tawny " ; *aureus*, " golden " ; *cereus*, " wax colour " ; *croceus*, " saffron colour " ; *sulphureus*, " sulphur colour " ; *buxeus*, " yellow as box-wood."

As to the Romans *courage* meant *endurance*, because the times they lived in were stern, so they had many words to express the idea of *cruelty*, as *crudelis*, " rough, unmerciful " ; *saevus*, " roused to fury " ; *ferus*, " savage by nature " ; *ferox*, sometimes meaning " courageous " but generally " savage " ; *durus*, " harsh," " unfeeling " ; while as a pleasure-loving people they had many words to express the idea of happiness, cheerfulness, and conviviality in varying degrees.

# NATIONALITY AND LANGUAGE 215

The Latin word for "home" is *domus*, which is connected with the idea of domination—the mastership over the household, while the *familia* was not our "family," but the whole number of slaves belonging to the *dominus*, or "master." The Romans could not get on without slaves, and we find many expressions used to show the light in which they were regarded.

*Servus* meant "a slave looked upon as a social inferior"; *famulus* was "one who formed a part of the household or *familia*"; a slave looked upon as a chattel that could be bought or sold was *mancipium*; *verna* was "a slave born in the household" and very often trained up as a jester; *puer* meant "a young boy slave," while *minister* and *ancilla* were names for male and female slaves looked upon merely as being able to serve.

In Rome's most glorious days, the family was a great institution, and the ties of relationship were considered very sacred, the Romans having many words to express relationships, even the most remote, and different words for paternal and maternal uncle, aunt, or cousin.

The Romans were a very methodical and logical people and liked to differentiate and mark small details and to give everybody and everything a name.

An old man past military age was *senex*, while an

old woman was not simply the feminine of this, but three separate words, each with a different meaning —*anus, anicula*, or *vetula*.

This love of classification is very well seen in the different words to denote the varying degrees of poverty or wealth that we have mentioned above. The word that would be used to correspond with our " millionaire " would be *rex*; *dives* would mean " rich," and *locuples* would be used to denote " ostentatious wealth "; *beatus* was used for " well-off," *opulentus* for " one who was powerful because rich." A person who was well-off and lucky was *fortunatus*, while one who had so much that he could give much to others was *abundans*.

The degrees of poverty were shown by such terms as *mendicus*, " having no money at all "; *egenus*, " having very little money "; *tenuis* meant " badly off," and was used of people who felt the pinch of poverty; *pauper* was used to denote people of small means who had only enough for moderate expenses; *inops* meant " destitute."

To the Englishman the word " home " is connected with the word "mother," so that we speak of our "mother tongue " and our " mother land," but the Roman's idea of home taught him to connect it with his father and to say *patria* = " fatherland," and *sermo patrius* = " father tongue."

The special characteristics of a nation can often be

## NATIONALITY AND LANGUAGE 217

seen in their choice of metaphors, and we find that the Romans frequently borrowed metaphors from agriculture, which had been the chief and honourable occupation of the early simple days; from military life, in which all men took part; from building, which became a mania with many Romans of later times; and from cookery, which is explained by the fondness of the people for feastings and dainty fare of all kinds.

Pork was a favourite dish; the swine is frequently referred to in plays, and many words occur in Latin for the many ideas that are connected with the care, cooking, and anatomy of this animal.

Perhaps the Romans' fondness for pork partly accounted for their scorn of the Jews who would not touch it.

The Latin equivalent for "to kill two birds with one stone" is *apros duos capere*, "to catch two wild boars," while a bungler or marplot was said "to let loose the boars among the fountains," *immittere fontibus apros*.

Words and expressions taken from agricultural life are *calamitas*, "calamity," first used of the destruction of crops; *cohors*, "a troop of soldiers," was in the first instance a "hedge"; *felix*, "happy," meant "fruit-bearing"; *pecunia*, "money," was connected with cattle; *deliro*, "I am deranged," meant originally "I go out of the furrow"; while "to do a thing awkwardly" was *arare bove asinoque*, "to plough with an ox and an ass."

Of words and expressions which belonged originally to military life we find a number, some such being *intervallum*, originally "the space between two palisades," but gradually coming to mean any "space"; *praemium*, "reward," first meant "profit gained from booty," just as *excellere* ("excel") originally meant "to shoot weapons at a mark." The Latin for "to sell by auction" was *sub hasta vendere* = "to sell under the spear," referring to the custom of selling captives directly after a victory; while "to make a mountain out of a mole-hill" was *arcem ex cloaca facere* = "to make a fortress out of a drain."

The Latin word for school was *ludus*, which also meant "game," "sport," and we get a glimpse of the gladiatorial schools and the fights in the Coliseum in the Latin equivalent for "labour lost," which is *operam et oleum perdere* = "to lose labour and oil," for the gladiators used much oil to keep themselves supple. The Greek original of our word "school" meant "leisure," "recreation."

We have mentioned in passing a few essential differences between the Greek and the Roman character, and the contrast between them is shown very clearly in their method of name-giving. The former loved to remember men distinguished as thinkers, poets, and philosophers, and gave nicknames expressive of

# NATIONALITY AND LANGUAGE

moral qualities, physical beauty, or intellectual superiority.

The Romans, however, preferred to remember the great soldiers who had served their country, and loved to recount and glorify the deeds of their ancestors on the field of battle, while their nicknames nearly always express contempt or refer to bodily or mental defects and are essentially prosaic.

Thus we have the names of military heroes such as Coriolanus who took Corioli, and of Scipio Africanus who won great glory in the struggle with Carthage in the North of Africa; but of the other class we have such examples as *Cicero* (wart), *Porcii* (pork), *Asini* (ass), *Varus* (bandy-legged), *Naso* (nosey), *Plancius* (broad-footed), *Balbus* (stutterer), *Flaccus*— the name of Horace the poet—(flap-eared).

Though the great empire of Rome has long since passed away, and though the language of its people is no longer spoken, surely it should not be called a " dead " language, as it often is, for a language that reflects the living character of the people who spoke it so many centuries ago, as clearly as Latin does, must be full of vitality itself.

But let us now come nearer home and see if we can tell at all the character of our early English ancestors by examining the language they used. We read in history books that the Anglo-Saxons were a wild and fierce race, fond of war and unaccustomed to settled life in towns. But history books, as we know them, were not written in these days, nor did people dream of putting down in so many words the character of their friends and foes, so that it is largely to the early literature, and the very words of the language itself, that we must go for information; and even if history said not a word about it, we could see clearly in the vocabulary of the Anglo-Saxons the impress of their character.

In reading Anglo-Saxon, or Early English, we are at once struck by the richness of the language—its wealth of synonyms, its vigour, its expressiveness, its poetic feeling.

We see before us a race just growing out of a state of chaos, grouping themselves into warrior tribes for the better preservation of life. This social chaos is reflected in the language by the expressions of passionate hate, of lust for revenge, of thirst for blood, of brutal ferocity, and of a certain childishness, all mingled with the staunchest loyalty and devotion and the most complete self-sacrifice, that are called forth by attachment to a common lord and leader.

We read in the *Anglo-Saxon Chronicle* of a certain *ætheling* (noble), Cyneheard, who rebelled against and surrounded a king named Cynewulf. The latter fought nobly to the last and fell fighting; the rebel leader then tried to buy the allegiance of the king's followers, with promises of land and money; but the royalists scorned the offer, saying that nothing was dearer to them than their lord, and that they would never follow his murderer, and they proved their loyalty by deeds, for they died fighting to a man.

This passionate loyalty to a leader and to a comrade is noticeable all through Anglo-Saxon literature; everywhere the hero is spoken of as a man of his word, a faithful friend, a loyal companion in arms, and a leader is called by such terms as *wise one, warden of the kingdom, treasure giver, ring giver, lord of men, friend of men, friendly lord, helmet of his people, safeguard of his people.*

The great virtues of the Anglo-Saxons were steadfastness in the " onslaught " and loyalty to his " shoulder-companion," while the enemy is described as the " wrathful breaker of pledges."

The battle-field was a training school for heroes; it taught the value of loyalty and friendship, strength of will and character, and developed the personality of its scholars by fostering nerve, self-reliance, and independence.

A hero must be " a wolf of war to foes," a " faithful shoulder-companion to his hearth-companions."

" Nothing can ever set aside friendship in him who is well-thinking," says one early writer, and again we read, " Wretched is he who deceives his friend," and " I know the people fast friends and firm foes."

Many words are used by the early writers for " friend," always a companion in arms in those warlike days—we have *shoulder-companion* (i.e. backer, close supporter), *health-companion, mead-companion, spear-comrade,* and others, and many words expressive of intimate and loyal affection between lord and thegns. A lord speaks (in the poem " Beowulf ") of a fallen thegn as " my counsellor, my adviser, my shoulder-companion when we guarded our heads in the onslaught . . . when the boar-head crests clashed together ; such as an earl should be, a good man and true, such was Æschere" ; and in the " Battle of Maldon" we read of an earl who died fighting for his lord, that " he lay dead beside his lord on the battle-field as a true man should," and in Anglo-Saxon the words " in a manner worthy of such a tie " are rendered by one very expressive adverb, *thegnlike*.

Another example of this feeling appears in the expression *thegn-sorrow* = " grief for the death of a thegn " ; *lord-sorrow,* " sorrow for the death of a lord," and so on, the use of such compounds having the effect of making the narrative intensely real and vivid.

As we have said, war was the chief occupation of our early forefathers and, among a people so fond of synonyms and metaphors as they were, we shall not be surprised to find twelve entirely different words for *fight*, thirty-seven for *hero* or *prince* (always a military leader), and any number for *sword, spear, arrow*, and the like.

A fight was *play of swords, clash of spears, the sword-drinking*, and many other paraphrases in addition to single words meaning " war " or " fight " ; while a spear was a *slaughter-shaft*, and a sword *the battle friend*, the *ringed* or *beaten iron*.

But our ancestors were not fighters on land only, they were sailors too, ready to encounter the perils of the deep, and the love of the sea and ships is a noticeable feature of their language and literature; so that we find many words for *sea* and *ship*, most of them poetical paraphrases, for they were poets at heart, these wild sea-rovers, and carried their poetry into their daily speech.

In the sea the Anglo-Saxon found the visible expression of the turmoil and tempest of his life—it seemed to him the image and embodiment of the conflict he saw all around him—he endowed it with a personality, as raging, as passionate, and untamed as himself. To him it was a monster of awe-inspiring aspect, an almost superhuman being, ever heaving with emotion, infuriated at times with passion akin to that which raged within his own breast. We read constantly of the *surging*, the *swaying,* the *boiling,* the *robbing,* the *strife* of the waves, and never of their gentler aspect. The sea was a mighty, treacherous enemy to be conquered—it called to conflict with a voice that appealed to all that was strong and valiant and enterprising in the English nature, and he exulted to know that he could conquer the foe and bring it into subjection.

What a contrast this to the attitude of the Roman!

Everywhere in our early literature we come upon fine pictures of the sea and of the launching of ships, of the embarking or disembarking of troops, of conflict with winds and waves. But always in these pictures Nature wears her sternest aspect—the sailing of ships is a strong man's sport; the atmosphere is always that of the open air, and the salt spray dashes us in the face as we read. We hear nothing but the roar of the storm, the boom of the waves, the cry of the gulls, and the bitter cold and frost and the " water-terror " freeze our very heart and soul.

Again and again we come across images taken from the sea and its life, for it expressed so well the restlessness that reigned in the sea-king's heart.

In a poem called " The Seafarer " we read, " Why crash together now the thoughts of my heart that I should try the salt waves' tumult? . . . he ever has longing who once sets out upon the sea."

The love of liberty, which he could indulge to the full on the trackless deep, was ingrained in the nature of the Anglo-Saxon. To him personal liberty, independence, and the realisation of his personality were all-important, and liberty was denied to no one but the very lowest—the serfs.

With all his independence and valour, the Anglo-Saxon was still a child at heart in many ways; he was very superstitious and believed firmly in charms and omens and in the supernatural; he was excitable, wanting in self-control, emotional and easily moved to tears. He was fond of home and family, and his wife was no slave or inferior, but the " peace-weaver," the " love-weaver." All through his valour, his deeds of prowess, and his frequent feastings in the " mead-hall," there runs a settled melancholy, a feeling of the transitoriness of earthly things, a realisation of the hidden sorrow of Nature, an unresisting acknowledgement of the hand of *Wyrd* or Fate that could not be evaded.

And had he no faults, this warrior-ancestor of ours ? Truly he had, and many. He cannot be acquitted of boastfulness at times, and, of course, he had the faults of his age—cruelty, revengefulness, and thirst for blood, though the literature that we possess—and it can be but a fragment, and that perhaps not the best—is a curious mixture of the old teaching " An eye for an eye, a life for a life," and the gentler " Love your enemies."

A lover of banquets and a deep drinker was this

hardy Norseman, and vivid pictures of feastings and drinking bouts, the resultant quarrels and riotous scenes, are to be found in the early poems. Then rang the mead-hall with shouts and the clashing of weapons, then was brandished the " spear-shaft," then was there " sword-play " and the ring of the " well-tempered war-friend " on byrnie and helm ; settles were overturned, shields were snatched from the walls, and the floor of the mead-hall " dinned " (echoed) with the tramp of the " weaponed men." This love of mead and ale seems to have been so great among the Anglo-Saxons that no celebration of any kind was possible without it—in fact, ale-drinking was the great feature of every occasion, as you will see when we say that a wedding or bridal was really a *bride-ale* or bride-drinking, *ale* being the usual name for a feast or gathering. So we hear of *church-ales*, *clerk-ales*, *scot-ales*, *bid-ales*, and you will probably think of *wassail*, which certainly is connected with the subject, for it now means " a health-drinking," but it does not contain the old word " ale " (*ealn*), but is from A.S. *wes* = " be thou," and *hāl*, " whole or in health."

But with all his faults the Anglo-Saxon was very lovable, and not least for his simplicity, his straightforwardness, and his poetry. The poet as well as the warrior was in every man, and all delighted in the song of the *shaper*, or minstrel, who was always at hand to add to the pleasure of a feast, or to celebrate some great victory in verse. The relief of *colour* is absent from the scenes we read of, for Nature herself was dull and grey, but the poetic touch ran through all in the choice of words and in the vividness of the word-pictures that have come down to us. The love of metaphor and synonym, both poetic traits, we have already noticed; in addition to this we might add such examples as the terms for the sea, which was called in turn *the whale's road, the swan road, sea road, sea streams,* while of a sailor we have the expressive compound *sea-weary.*

A ship was called *sea-wood, ringed prow,* from the custom of hanging shields round the fore part, while inanimate objects were personified and endowed with names, as in the case of the famous sword *Hrunting* of which we read in "Beowulf," the forerunner of King Arthur's Excalibur and the celebrated Durendal of Roland.

The Anglo-Saxons knew no law but that of the sword, and their art seems to have been confined to the decoration of helmets, byrnies, and weapons, and the adorning of their mead-halls with trophies of war. Frequent allusions are made to the decorations on swords and to the marvellous skill of the smiths, but we do not know what these decorations consisted of; but Hrothgar, the king of whom we read in "Beowulf" had a hall called *Heorot* because adorned with the horns of stags.

Relics of some of the customs of those early days are still with us, as in the christening of a ship with wine, corresponding to the reddening of the wheels of the rollers with blood at the launching of a ship. Now, at the funeral of an officer in the army, his horse is led behind the coffin, a custom which is a legacy from the times when a warrior's horse was killed and buried with him that he might not go steedless into the other world.

Thus were our Anglo-Saxon forefathers as seen in their language. Much more might be said, but perhaps we have seen enough to prove that national character can be read in language and to show that in learning a foreign tongue we are doing more than learning tiresome lists of words and mastering grammatical rules; we are forging for ourselves a key to many riddles that history cannot else solve and putting ourselves in touch with the living personality of those who have long since passed away, so that we may say of them that they being dead, yet speak.

# BIBLIOGRAPHY

THERE are not many elementary books on the subject of language in general, but an excellent introduction is Sweet's *History of Language* (Temple Primer, 1901) and the article on Philology in the *Encyclopædia Britannica*.

Whitney's *Language and the Study of Language* (1875) and his *Life and Growth of Language* (1886), though necessarily out of date in some ways, contain much that is valuable and that will always hold good. A more advanced book is Tucker's *The Natural History of Language*. Two interesting French books (both translated) are Darmesteter's *The Life of Words* (1886), dealing chiefly with French, but of general interest also; and Bréal's *Semantics* (1900), the first book to deal systematically with the science of *meanings*.

Among books treating of the beginnings of language, Tylor's *Anthropology* (1881) and Lord Avebury's *Origin of Civilisation* (1912) both contain interesting chapters on the subject; and in *Prehistoric Man* (1913), also by Lord Avebury, can be found an account of the Cave Men. Professor Max Müller's

*Lectures on the Science of Language* also deal with the subject in greater detail.

For the history of writing and the alphabet a chapter in Tylor's *Anthropology* is again useful and simple, and for a more detailed treatment of the subject Clodd's *Story of the Alphabet* (1900). *The Beginnings of Writing* (1895), by Hoffman, treats chiefly of the picture writing of the American Indians; Tucker (above) has a chapter on the subject, while *The Alphabet* by Canon Isaac Taylor (1883) is very full.

Of books on the English language there are legion. Among the more useful and elementary are Bradley's excellent *The Making of English* (1904), *The Growth of English*, by Wyld (1907), and *The History of the English Language* (1910), by O. F. Emerson; while more advanced books are Wyld's *The Historical Study of the Mother Tongue* (1907) (dealing largely with phonetics), Jespersen's *Progress in Language* (1894) and his *Growth and Structure of the English Language*, both interesting as the judgment of a foreign scholar.

Though the *New English Dictionary* has put many of the etymologies out of court, Archbishop Trench's books *English Past and Present* and *On the Study of Words* are still suggestive; while more modern books which deal chiefly with the vocabulary of English are *Words and their Ways in English Speech* (1902), by Greenough and Kittredge ; *The Romance of Words* (1912), by Ernest Weekley; and *The English Language*, by L. Pearsall Smith.

For etymology there are Skeat's *Principles of English Etymology* (1892), Sweet's *New English Grammar*, and, for those who cannot consult the *New English Dictionary*, Skeat's *Concise Etymological English Dictionary* (1911).

Shakespearean grammar can be studied in Abbot's book with that title (1870), and accidence in Morris's *Historical Outline of English Accidence*, 1895.

The *Romance of Names* (1914), by Ernest Weekley, treats very interestingly of names both personal and geographical. *Family Names and their Story* (1909), by S. Baring-Gould, and the *Homes of Family Names in Great Britain* (1890), by H. B. Guppy, go fully into the subject ; *Place Names of England and Wales* (1915), by J. B. Johnston, is the latest authority; while *Words and Places*, by Isaac Taylor, though out of date in many respects, is suggestive, and his chapter on " English Village Names " is sound and thorough.

Of books on Language and Character there are few, and none of an elementary nature. One little book by Professor Moulton, *Two Lectures on the Science of Language* (1903), is useful as an introduction to the study of language generally and deals briefly with the Aryan question. Isaac Taylor's *The Origin of the Aryans* (1889), dealing to some extent with ethnology, is necessarily somewhat out of date, especially as to etymology, but is very readable and can be checked by the larger *Prehistoric Antiquities of the Aryan Peoples* by O. Schrader, translated by Dr. F. B. Jevons (1890). Weise's *Language and Character of the Roman People* is also translated into English.

# INDEX

## A

acre, 123
Adelaide, 156
adverbs, old and modern forms, 113-14
adjectives, old and modern forms, 106; comparative and superlative of, 107
advertise, 123
alphabet, history of the, 26 sqq.; myths of origin, 28; Anglo-Saxon, 45; Greek, 44; Phœnician, 43-4; Roman, 44-5; (see also Runes, Ogham)
analytic language, 77-8, 91
angel, 59, 118
Anglo-Saxon, alphabet, 45; elements in English, 57-8, 75 sqq., 91, 102 sqq., 109 sqq., 128; pronunciation, 86; dialects, 80 sqq.; national characteristics in language, 219 sqq.
Anglo-Saxon Chronicle, the, 82
animals, names of, from places, 175; metaphors from, 146; personal names from, 186; place names from, 178
anomalies, 117 sqq.
Arabic, 14; numerals, 44
arrant, 126
art of the Cave Men, 3
Aryan people, 11, 19; racial characteristics in language, 197 sqq. (see Mother Language)
Assyrian inscriptions, 28, 35

atlas, 191
attic, 136
auxiliary verbs, 111-12
Avestas, 17, 18
avon (afon), 158
awful, 121

## B

bacon (save one's), 121
Baltic (see Slavonic group)
banisters (balusters), 132
barricade, 70
Basque, 14
battledore, 70
Battle of Maldon, the, 82
bed-ridden, 132
belfry, 132
Beowulf, 82, 227
Bible, English of the, 90, 108, 109; metaphors from, 150; personal names from, 187
binnacle, 71
birds, 124
Black Letter printing, 48
bland, 125
bobbies, 190
book, 27
Book of the Dead, 34, 40
Breton, 12, 24; elements in English, 57
bridal, 226
burg (burgh), etc., 165
butcher, 122

## C

cab, 129
calico, 176

233

cambric, 176
cannibal, 176
canter, 129, 177
carking, 139
Carlisle, 161
Carlyle's English, 72, 101, 107
case-endings in Old English, 83, 99, 103-4, 106, 113
cashmere, 176
Cave Dwellers, 2 sqq.
Celtic languages, 13, 24; elements in English, 56-7
Celtic place names, in Britain, 157 sqq.
Chaldean inscriptions, 39
chancellor, 135
changes of meaning, 117 sqq., 129
changes of word-form through sound-laws, 126 sqq.; through ignorance, 130 sqq.
chapman, 183
Chaucer's English, 64-5, 77, 85, 87, 109, 130
cherry, 175
children's language, 5, 9
Chinese, 14; alphabet, 28, 35; words in English, 73
Christian, 119
Christian names, 179
Church, the, words borrowed from, 59, 62
churl, 119
climate, influence of, on language, 193-4
clog almanac, 32
cobalt, 72
coco-nut, 70
comparative (adjectival) endings, 107
conjunctions, English, origin of, 115
copper, 124
costermonger, 135
court cards, 136
crack, 7, 140
crafty, 121
cuneiform writing, 28, 35 sqq.
cunning, 121

cursive (Roman) writing, 45
Cymric, 13, 24
cynic, 136
Czech, 23

D

Danish, 13, 55; elements in English, 60-1, 80, 82, 86; place names in England, 167 sqq.
dapper, 125
dative case in Old English, 99, 104
days of the week, names, 103-4, 191
decimate, 122
dialect, not debased speech, 95-6; of capital city as national standard, 21, 22 (see London)
dialects, ancient Greek, 20; old English, 80 sqq.; modern English, 96-7, 130
disaster, 134
doublets (see synonyms)
Dover, 161
"Dream of the Rood, the," 52, 81-2
Dryden's English, 89, 101, 108
dumps, the, 121
Dutch, 12, 25; elements in English, 71

E

Early English (see Anglo-Saxon)
East Midland dialect, 84
Egypt, ancient, inscriptions, 39 sqq.
Eisteddfod, the, 24
Elizabethan English (see Shakespeare)
Ember days, 131
English, affinities with other tongues, 13, 54 sqq.; elements in, of Anglo-Saxon, 56 sqq., 91; Celtic, 56-7; Latin, 57 sqq., 67-8; ecclesiastical introductions, 59, 62; analysis of elements, 60, 91; elements and influence of

# INDEX

Danish, 60-1, 80, 82, 86; of Norman-French, 61 sqq., 80, 83, 128-9; of French, 55, 64-5, 92, 101; of the Renaissance, 67 sqq.; of Greek, 68; of Italian, 59, 69; of Spanish and Portuguese, 70; of Dutch, 71; of German, 72; of other foreign tongues, 72-3; historic development and change, 75 sqq.; Shakespeare's 87 sqq., 98 sqq.; modern, 77, 90, 94; "good," 94; standard, 95; pronunciation of, 97-8; grammatical variations, 98, 103 sqq.; periods, Romantic, Classical, Augustan, 101 (see also dialects, inflections)
English people, national characteristics in language, 219 sqq.
Erse, 13, 24; elements in English, 57
exorbitant, 123
extravagant, 123

## F

fable, 124
Falconer, 185
fearful, 121
Feudal System, words from, 62
fetish, 70
Finnish, 14
flap, 7, 139
fond, 118
ford, in place names, 167
foreign words, in English, 72-3
French, 13, 22; influence and elements in English, 55, 61 sqq., 80, 83, 84, 92, 101; characteristics, 127 sqq.; national traits in, 196
fret, 139
Frisian, 25
furlong, 123
futhorc, 51

## G

Gaelic, 13, 24; elements in English, 57

gallon, 123
garden, 123
gauntlet (run the), 146
genitive case, in Old English, 103-4, 113
geographical names (see place); for plants, animals, etc., 175 sqq.
German (High, Low), 13, 25; influence on English, 71
gesture, in speech, 4 sqq.
girl, 124
glass, 124
" good English," 94
gooseberry, 135
gossip, 120
Gothic, 25; alphabet, 52
Greek, 13, 44; origin and spread, 19 sqq.; dialects of, 20; characteristics of, 195, 197; national traits in, 207
greensward, 125
gull, 148

## H

half, 106
hall, in place names, 165
ham, in place names, 164
handwriting, 45, 50
hansom, 190
heathen, 135
Hebrew, 14, 44; words in English, 73
herd, in surnames, 185
Hindu, ancient (see Sanskrit); modern, English words from, 73
horn book, the, 49
House, the, 124
humble pie, 131
huzzy, 121

## I

Icelandic, 13
idea, 122
ideographic writing, 29, 33 sqq.
ill-starred, 134
illumination of MSS., 47
imp, 119

Indo-European, 13 (see Mother Language)
infinitive forms, 109
inflections in Old English, 75; disappearance of, 76 sqq., 83, 87, 103 sqq.
influence, 122, 134
ing, in place names, 165-6
instrumental case, the, 106
interjections, 195
Irish (see Erse)
iron, 124
Italian, 13, 22, 23; influence on English, 69; characteristics of, 126, 195
italics, 177
its, 108

**J**

jaunt, 121
jersey, 176
" Jerusalem " artichoke, 131
Johnson's English, 101-2
Jones, Sir W., 18
Jonson, Ben, 108, 109
jovial, 134

**K**

knave, 119
knightly, 125

**L**

lady, 134
language, origin and growth of, 2 sqq.
languages, European (see Mother Language); non-European, 14
Latin, 13; origin and spread, 21 sqq.; influence on English, 57 sqq., 67-8; national characteristics in, 207 sqq.; popular, 22; alphabet, 44
legion, 122
ley (lea), in place names, 165
libel, 119
Lithuanian, 13, 16, 23
little, 106
local names (see place)
London, 160
London, dialect of, the national standard, 22, 77, 84, 87

Londonderry, 156
lord, 134
lumber, 176

**M**

macadam, 191
malapert, 125
Malay words in English, 73
Manx, 13, 24
marshal, 118
martyr, 59, 118
Maryborough, 156
meander, 191
meerschaum, 72
mer, in place names, 165
Mercian (see Midland)
mercurial, 134
metaphors, 137 sqq.; from animals, 146; archery, 143; the Bible, 150; chivalry, 145; the classics, 151; colour, 149; fables, 151; music, 152; seafaring, 142-3; sport, 148; war, 145
Methodist, 119
mews, 149
Middle English, 77, 92
Midland (Mercian) dialect, 81, 84-5, 87, 94, 104
milliner, 177
minister, 59, 118
mint, 134
miss, 129
mnemonic records, 29 sqq.
Modern English, 77, 90, 94
money, 134, 199, 209
months, names of, 191
Mother Language, European, 10, 13 sqq., 23; word-relationships in, 17, 23; characteristics, 197 (see also Greek, Latin, Roman, Celtic, Teutonic)
mountains, names of, 160 sqq.

**N**

names, personal, 179 sqq.; Roman, 219; common nouns from, 190 (see surnames)

# INDEX

national character, traits of, in language, 193 sqq.
nice, 118
nicknames, as surnames, 186; Roman, 219
Niebuhr, K., 37
noddle, 121
Norman-French (see French); place names in Britain, 174
Norse place names in Britain, 166 sqq.
Northumbrian dialect, 81 sqq.
Norwegian, 13, 25
numerals, Arabic, 44; Roman, 44

## O

Ogam alphabet, 52-3
Old English (see Anglo-Saxon)
onomatopœic words, 6 sqq., 139-40

## P

pagan, 135
paper, 27
paradise, 118
parchment, 176
Paris, dialect of, the national standard, 21
participle, past, old and modern forms, 111; present, old and modern forms, 110
pate, 121
peach, 175
pen (or ben), in place names, 161
penmanship, art of, 50
Penn wampum, the, 30
pert, 125
petrel, 192
phaeton, 191
Philipstown, 156
Phœnicians, the, 43
phonetic writing, 29, 35, 40
pictorial writing, 29, 32-3
place names, Celtic, 156 sqq.; Early English, 164 sqq.; Norman-French, 174; Norse and Danish, 166 sqq.; Roman, 162 sqq.; Saxon, 163; descriptive

of size, position, etc., 177-8; significance of, 155 sqq.
plants, names of, from places, 175; from persons, 190
pluck, 126
plural forms in English, 84, 104-5
point, metaphorical usage, 140
Polish, 13, 23; English words from, 72
Pope's English, 89, 101
Portuguese, 13, 22, 23, elements in English, 70
prepositions, English, origin of, 115
preposterous, 122
prevaricate, 133
printing, invention of, influence on language, 85, 87
privilege, 122
pronouns, English, inflected, 108
pronunciation of Old English, 86; varieties of, in modern English, 97, 130
Provençal, 23
provincial English (see dialect)
Prussian, Old, 23

## Q

quaint, 125
Quaker, 119
Quipus, Peruvian, 30
quixotic, 192

## R

rather, 107
Rawlinson, Sir H., 37
reasty, 125
rebus, 34
reclaim, 149
Red Indian records, 30, 33; words in English, 73
Renaissance, the, influence on English, 67 sqq.
restive, 124
Rig-Veda, the, 15
Rhodesia, 156
rhubarb, 175
rivers, names of, 157 sqq.
rod (pole, perch), 123

# INDEX

Roman language (see Latin)
Roman people, national characteristics in languages, 207 sqq;
Roman place names in Britain, 162 sqq.
Romance languages, 13, 22, 197
Rome, dialect of, the national standard, 21
roots, 124
Rosetta Stone, the, 41
Roumanian, 13, 22
Runes, 28, 51 sqq.
Russian, 13, 23, 44; English words from, 72
rusty, 124
Ruthwell cross, the, 52, 81

## S

sacrament, 59, 118
Sagas, the, 25
salary, 145
salt cellar, 131
Sanskrit, 13, 15, 197
saturnine, 134
Scandinavian group, 13, 25
scientific terminology, 68
Scottish (see Gaelic)
Scriptorium, the, 46
sea, the, in ancient language, 205, 211, 223, 227; metaphors from, 142–3
Seafarer, the, 82
sexton, 120
Shakespeare's English, 87 sqq. 98 sqq., 107, 108, 109, 113, 118, 143, 147; pronunciation of, 88
shrewd, 118
sight (multitude), 121
signs for language, 4 sqq.
silly, 120
skip, 121
Slavonic group, 13, 23
Smith, 183
smug, 125
Sodor and Man, 171
sound-laws, 18, 127
Southern (West-Saxon) dialect, 81, 94, 104

Spanish, 13, 22, 23; elements in English, 70; characteristics, 195–6
spelling, English, unsystematic, 93–4
Spenser's English, 110–11, 119
standard English, 95 sqq., 101
stentorian, 191
steward, 118
stocking, 133
style (stylus), 27
supercilious, 136
superlative (adjectival) endings, 107
surnames, origin of, 179 sqq.; Anglo-Saxon, 181; Jewish, 180; Norman-French, 183; Roman, 219; derived from animals, 186; Christian names, 186; colours, 186; nicknames, 186, 219; places, 182; sports, 185; trades, 183 sqq., 189; the mother, 188; peculiar to districts, 188 sqq.; common nouns, formed from, 190
Sutherland, 168
sward, 126
Swedish, 13
synonyms, 64 sqq.
synthetic language, 77–8, 91

## T

tallies, 31
tantalise, 151, 191
tartar, 176
tawdry, 192
tenses in Anglo-Saxon, 109
terrible, 121
Teutonic languages, 13, 25, 197, 205 sqq.
thorpe, in place names, 166
thwaite, in place names, 166
ton (town), 164–5
tor, 161
town names, 161 sqq.
treacle, 133
triumph, 122
trivial, 132

trounce, 121
Truro, 161
Turkish, English words from, 72
tweed, 176

## U

Ulphilas, Bp., 25, 52
uncial writing, 45
unique, 126

## V

Vedas, the, 15, 18
verbs, in Old English, 109-10; auxiliary, 111-12; formed from adverbs, 114
Vercelli MS., 81
Vikings (see Norse)
villain, 119
volume, 27
vulgar, 123

## W

wampum records, 30
Wansdyke, 156
ward, in surnames, 185
wassail, 226

Welsh, 13, 24; elements in English, 57
West Saxon (Wessex) dialect, 81, 87
which, 108
who, 108
Widsith, 82
willy-nilly, 112
wines, named from localities, 175
words, life-histories of, 117 sqq.; changes of meaning, 118 sqq. changes of sound and form, 127 sqq.
worsted, 176
worthy, 125
Wycliffe's English, 85

## Y

yard, 123
York, 161

## Z

Zend, 13, 15, 17, 197
Zend-Avestas, 17
Zoroaster, 18

www.ingramcontent.com/pod-product-compliance
Lightning Source LLC
Chambersburg PA
CBHW020327170426
43200CB00006B/297